Perfect Puppy in Seven Days:
How to Start Your Puppy Off Right

By Sophia Yin, DVM, MS

Copyright ©2011 by Sophia A. Yin
Library of Congress Control Number: 2011910827
ISBN: 978-0-9641518-7-1

Editor: Beth Adelman
Proofreader: Donna Dyer
Photographers: Sophia Yin and Melissa Morris
Graphic Designers: Larry Peters and April Kimmerly (www.pkcreate.com)
Illustrator: Lili Chin (www.doggiedrawings.net)

Disclaimer
The publisher and the author make no representation or warranties with respect to the accuracy or completeness of the contents of this work and specifically disclaim all warranties, including without limitation warranties of fitness for a particular purpose. No warranty may be created or extended by sales or promotional materials. The advice and strategies contained herein may not be suitable for every situation. This work is sold with the understanding that the publisher is not engaged in rendering legal, veterinary, or other professional services. If professional assistance is required, the services of a competent professional person should be sought. Neither the publisher nor the author shall be liable for damages arising heretofore. The fact that an organization or web site is referred to in this work as a citation and/or a potential source of further information does not mean that the author or the publisher endorses the information that the organization or web site may produce or recommendations it may make. Further, readers should be aware that Internet web sites listed in this work may have changed or disappeared between when this work was written and when it was read.

For free information as well as to view other products by Dr. Sophia Yin, go to www.drsophiayin.com.

CattleDog Publishing
P.O. Box 4515
Davis, CA 95617-4516
Email: Info@drsophiayin.com
Fax (530) 757-2383
www.drsophiayin.com
(888) 638-9989

Introduction

Chapter 5: Dr. Sophia Yin's Learn to Earn Program for Puppies.

Dedication

For all of the older dogs who liked the household better before it had a new puppy.

Praise for Perfect Puppy in 7 Days

Raising a puppy successfully takes patience and dedication but the process can be made a whole lot easier by reading Sophia Yin's excellent book, *Perfect Puppy in 7 Days*. Packed with the latest information, Dr. Yin takes the reader into the puppy's world, helping them to not only understand a puppy's developmental process, but giving useful tips and techniques to ensure that any puppy becomes a happy, confident adult. This book is a must-have for any puppy parent or canine educator.

–Victoria Stilwell
Dog trainer, author and host of Animal Planet's *It's Me or the Dog*

This is like no other puppy book you've seen before. With over 400 photos it visually takes you through the steps needed to potty train, socialize, and provide your puppy with life skills. And it ensures that your puppy will enjoy behaving well, because it teaches owners how to make good behavior fun. It's not just about teaching your puppy manners, it's a step-by-step recipe for bonding with your puppy, learning to communicate with him, and preparing you pup for life! With Dr. Yin's approach your puppy will learn more in a week than many dogs learn in a year!

–Dr. Marty Becker
"America's Veterinarian"
Resident veterinarian on Good Morning America and The Dr. Oz Show
Author of 20 pet books including "Your Dog: The Owner's Manual"

This book is a comprehensive and humane guide to puppy behavior and training, incorporating a detailed guide on how to interpret your puppy's body language. Worth buying for the socialization advice and checklist alone.

– John Bradshaw, Ph. D.
Director of the University of Bristol's Anthrozoology Institute
Author of *Dog Sense: How the New Science of Dog Behavior Can Make you a Better Friend to Your Pet*

Well written, factually correct and brilliantly illustrated. I would not hesitate to recommend it to anyone thinking of getting a new puppy. Two paws up for a great contribution!

–Dr. Nicholas Dodman, Director of the Animal Behavior Clinic at Tufts Cummings School
of Veterinary Medicine

This well-organized book is filled with essential information about puppy development and learning. Experts and novices alike will appreciate the illustrations and analogies that turn science into a clear and enjoyable read. Most important, Dr. Yin offers a plan that incorporates critical socialization and training into a daily routine. It will be a puppy life-saver.

–Ellen M. Lindell, VMD, Dip ACVB
Veterinary Behavior Consultations, P.C., Pleasant Valley, NY

I own tons of dog training books and none of them are as much fun to read as this one. It's accurate and easy to access. The graphics and text work together to explain all of the concepts that Dr. Yin lays out. The puppy socialization chapters and checklist are especially well done. If you have a puppy, work with puppies, raise puppies, or just plain like puppies, get this book.

–Nancy Abplanalp CPDT-KA and Education Specialist
Thinking Dogs
www.thinkingdogs.net

I am thrilled with the *Perfect Puppy in 7 Days!* As a professional dog trainer, I am always searching for reward-based resources for my clients, especially first time puppy owners. This book lays out, in detail, how to set your puppy up for success from Day 1 using common sense, gentle techniques, while establishing clear communication between puppy and person. I am recommending this book to all puppy owners!

–Jenn Merrit, CPDT-KA
Tellington TTouch Companion Animal Practitioner
APDT Professional Member
Blue Dog Creature Coaching, Efland, NC

I love Dr. Yin's approach as it is not only easy to understand, but is also easy to follow! I have two Shiba Inus, who are supposed to be one of the most difficult breeds, and this approach works well for us even though I am a first time dog owner! Get this book and you will set your puppy up for success with a solid foundation to live happily and harmoniously with you.

–Sandra Tung
Happy Pet Pawrent of 2 Shiba Inus

Introduction

If you'd asked me a year ago what I'd be doing the summer of 2009, I guarantee I would not have guessed I'd be training a puppy for my dad. But several months earlier I'd had some premonitions that this might be coming up. »

First, my parents' Scottie, Meggie (Figure A), got splenic lymphosarcoma. She had her spleen removed and subsequently seemed perfectly healthy. But the initial scare put an idea in my dad's head. He was hinting that he wanted to add another dog to the family. When I would visit them—they live 85 miles away—with my Jack Russell Terrier, Jonesy (Figure B), my dad would slip in statements like, "Let me have Jonesy," or "Jonesy's mine."

Fig. A
Meggie

Fig. B
Jonesy

Okay, anyone who knows Jonesy, the $300,000 dog, knows the only way he would live with someone else would be over my dead body. He's known to my friends as the $300,000 dog because of the number of hours of training I've put in with him over the last five years. And that's just so that he can function like a normal, well-behaved dog in day-to-day life. He was so bad that in spite of his apparently fantastic behavior when working with me, all of my dog training assistants who worked with Jonesy that first year and a half decided they would never get a Jack Russell Terrier—at least not one like him.

Now fast-forward several months. Meggie did phenomenally well after her surgery. For months she was running around like a Mazda Miata with a new transmission. But eventually the lymphosarcoma came back. We had to put poor Meggie to sleep.

Some people need a few weeks to grieve before they get another pet. Some people need a lot longer. Others need a pet at all times. My dad, it turns out, is one of the latter. Not a week had gone by before my dad was demanding, "Get me an Australian Cattle Dog. One just like my last Cattle Dog, Roody" (Figures C and D).

Fig. C
Roody

Fig. D
Roody as a puppy

Why an Australian Cattle Dog (ACD)—a dog known by many to have a tendency to herd, nip and bite? Their reputation is so infamous in some circles that a fellow veterinarian who worked in Australia once told me, "When you drive to a farm, never get out of the car if there's a goose or an Australian Cattle Dog."

Why an Australian Cattle Dog? Because 20 years ago when I didn't know any better, I'd bought him an ACD puppy who we named Roody. According to my dad, Roody was the perfect dog—like a canine combination of Einstein and Gandhi.

I have to admit that Roody was the perfect companion. Starting at 12 weeks of age, he always stuck close to us, was magically calm as a puppy—no mouthing or incessant playing—and he practically self–potty trained. He was also extremely eager, which made him appear pretty smart. Mostly he just tried things over and over at the speed of light until one of his attempts turned out right. There wasn't a whole lot of thinking involved there.

What my dad forgets about Roody is that he used to bark ballisticly when people or dogs approached the car, and snapped at dogs who came too close. My parents just sort of avoided the problem situations.

And I remember when my roommate in veterinary school borrowed Roody for the UC Davis Picnic Day Parade to walk alongside our class's float. Although Roody knew how to heel nicely for me, he hadn't had consistent training from my parents. So for them and others he bounced around in different directions like a Kong® toy on an elastic rope. And then there was the description by a family friend when referring to Roody's rude treat-grabbing skills (as trained by my dad): "Everyone knows that when giving treats to Roody, he gets the whole beef jerky."

Of course, there was no way my dad would listen to me or my mom warning him that Roody wasn't as perfect as he remembered and that another Cattle Dog wouldn't be just like Roody anyway. I had even owned a second ACD, Zoe, who was clearly very different from Roody. She was great with people and dogs, for one. But my dad only had Roody in his mind when he thought Australian Cattle Dog.

Old Dogs Can Learn New Tricks, but Old Humans Are Set in Their Ways.

When Roody was 13, my parents traded him to me for the younger Meggie. At that age Roody could still hang with me on 10-mile runs and play Frisbee. And I quickly trained him to be friendly around other dogs and take treats nicely. Despite his age, the training was easy because dogs will do whatever behavior is rewarded, as long as the old behaviors no longer work.

Humans, on the other hand, can be set in their ways. My mom and I knew that at 81 years of age, my dad wasn't about to change his mind or his ways. Either I was going to get him a Cattle Dog, or my mom would come home one day to one that my dad found on a whim. My dad wanted a Cattle Dog just like Roody and he wanted one now!

The Race to Find the Right Puppy.

So my assistant, Melissa, and I perused the web for available ACDs, assuming I wouldn't find one who looked just like Roody for months. And then out of the blue, there was a litter of puppies available nearby and their photos were posted on the web. There was one female available. Her parents were OFA-certified fair and good, tested negative for progressive retinal atrophy, and the female puppy looked close enough to Roody to be acceptable to my dad.

Even more important to me when I visited was her behavioral health. Her parents were both friendly to humans—no crazy nipping at the heels or defensive postures. Plus she was curious but polite when she greeted the test dog I brought with me. So I reserved her for my dad and picked her up several days later when she was 8 weeks of age and just before the rest of her siblings would be leaving to their new homes.

In fact, I got her several days before my dad knew. That way I would have time to start training her without listening to his incessant nagging to drop everything I was doing and bring his puppy to him. My goal was to start her socialization to people and dogs and to train her through the puppy Learn to Earn program in a week, so that she would already have good habits before my dad got her. That way he'd have less chance to mess her up.

How This Book Came About.

I have to admit, I was not looking forward to having a pup, dealing with potty training and putting up with the busybody nature of a puppy. But it turned out that in her first week with me, Lucy (that's the name my Dad gave her even before he had her) learned to be perfect. By the end of the week, she was automatically sitting to greet people, to go in and out of the house, to get her

Fig. E

Lucy running with her littermates: These puppies are racing after their mom for a meal. The mom is high-tailing it in the other direction trying to keep away. At seven weeks of age their teeth hurt!

These puppies are mature compared to many other breeds of puppy their age. They can already run around for prolonged periods without getting tired.

leash on and basically every time she wanted something from me or we were walking and I stopped. She met about 10 dogs and played nicely with them, but also came when called. And she loved all the people she met.

To me she seemed the like the easiest puppy ever. But my assistant kept telling me she's the same as all the other puppies she and I have worked with and that I just like Australian Cattle Dogs, so I was imagining Lucy was better.

Anyway, regardless of how good she was for me, the ultimate goal was that she learn to be polite for my parents, too. That meant they needed to learn the techniques I had used as quickly as possible, without me being present to tutor them through it. So I created a book illustrated with 250+ photos for them to use. This book. Since then, I have revised and added even more photos and information.

I hope you enjoy the photos and the reading. By following the steps illustrated in this book, you'll quickly develop a clear line of communication with your new companion and be on the way to developing your own perfect pup.

The Purpose of This Book.

This book is a step-by-step guide for understanding and communicating with your puppy, so you can teach good habits quickly while forming a strong, trusting relationship. It provides the basics of reading body language and understanding perception as well as a comprehensive guide for making desirable behavior a habit rather than a trick performed only when food is present.

" I was not looking forward to having a pup, dealing with potty training and putting up with the busy body nature of a puppy. But it turned out that in her first week with me, Lucy learned to be perfect. "

Chapter 1

How Your Puppy Developed Before You Got Her

Typically, pet owners don't interact with a new puppy until they bring her home at 8-12 weeks of age. But what happens even before then, during the first precious weeks, can affect her for the rest of her life. »

Lack of exposure to a variety of people before 12 weeks of age can result in fear of unfamiliar humans, being raised as a single puppy can lead to impaired social skills, and being raised by an anxious or timid mother can result in puppies who are more withdrawn. In fact, while many people assume that fearful dogs are so scared because they must have been abused in the past, it's far more common that the cause is lack of adequate early socialization.

From health, to interactions with littermates, to the richness of her early environment, it's essential that the puppy's breeder or early caretaker take an active role in shaping the puppy's behavioral health. And to do that, they must understand normal puppy development and perception. It will be useful for you to understand, as well.

1.1 The Neonatal Period (0 to 14 Days).

A puppy is born deaf and blind, and immediately after birth has one mission—to find warmth and food. She instinctively pulls herself in the direction of any heat source while reflexively rooting her nose whenever it touches an object. Once she finds the warm underside of her mother, her rooting pays off as she grasps a nipple and starts sucking in the warm, antibody-rich milk.

During the first two weeks, puppies spend most of their time sleeping huddled with their littermates, with brief interruptions for nursing. Most of their sleep is REM or stage IV sleep—a stage characterized by involuntary twitching and high brain activity. One reason puppies sleep in a heap is that they have no shivering reflex or insulating fat. That means a healthy newborn can only maintain a body temperature about 12°F above her environment. In fact, her core body temperature won't hit its normal of 101.5°F until she is about four weeks old.

Her ability to regulate her temperature improves by about three and a half weeks old, and then puppies tend to sleep side by side instead of in a heap. Later on they may sleep more spread out. But even so, puppies and dogs often choose to sleep in contact with a wall, object, or person.

At this age, only three of their five senses are working—touch, taste and smell—and even these are not fully developed. With only a fraction of their senses functioning, puppies do not yet exhibit signs of fear of their environment. However, they do respond to pain, discomfort, and minor disturbances by whining.

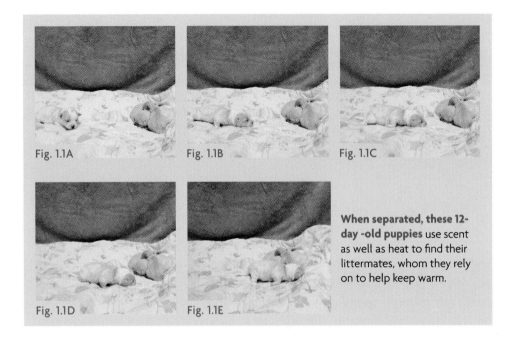

Fig. 1.1A   Fig. 1.1B   Fig. 1.1C

Fig. 1.1D   Fig. 1.1E

When separated, these 12-day -old puppies use scent as well as heat to find their littermates, whom they rely on to help keep warm.

1.1.1 Touch and handling.

Changes in temperature or little disturbances—hunger, human handling and body position changes brought on by the movement of siblings or the mother—can upset neonates. As humans, our first instinct is to provide a completely protective and stress-free environment. However, some exposure to these stressors is important for puppies' development. A little stress early on helps them develop the ability to cope with real life.

That's why the neonatal period is an ideal time to start handling the puppies for short amounts of time. Feeling the ears, feet, tail and mouth, and holding them in different positions for even 30 seconds to several minutes a day may greatly decrease their stress and reactivity to handling. Changes in their reactions can be seen within a week or less. The amount and type of handling may need to be tailored, based on the puppy's response as she matures.

1.1.2 Taste.

Puppies can detect taste as soon as they are born, and can show taste preferences early on. Once they start moving around at about three weeks old, they will explore food items in their environment.

This particular puppy has been handled for 30 seconds a day, starting at 3 days of age. By 14 days of age she no longer whines or struggles when held in different positions. Lucy's breeder has also taken care to handle Lucy and the other puppies in her litter, which will help Lucy accept everyday interactions such as grooming, towel-drying wet feet, and other daily care with ease.

Fig. 1.1.1A

1.1.3 Smell, sensitivity, and discrimination.

Dogs have 10 times more surface area within the nose with which to detect smells and 100 times more brain cells dedicated to their sense of smell than humans. Even as a neonate, a pup's sense of smell is better than ours. While the sense may not be fully developed, as the puppy matures her superior scenting ability will open up a world that humans are unable to perceive. She will grow up to have the ability to detect a drop of scent diluted in an Olympic-size pool of water, the potential to smell cancer on the breath of a human, and the ability to distinguish between individual human odors even of identical twins if both twins are present for comparison.

Fig. 1.1.3A

A puppy's superior sense of smell opens up a world that humans are unable to perceive.

1.2 Vision Starts at the End of the Neonatal Period.

Although the eyelids open at 10 to 14 days of age, the young puppy's vision is poor at first. The puppy can follow objects and respond to movement, but her vision is not sharp. The acuity will improve some, but even as adults, dogs don't have especially sharp vision. They don't need to read newspapers or street signs. And because they are much lower to the ground than humans, smell and hearing can be more useful in finding food and sensing danger, since scents and sounds can travel around objects that might block their view.

1.2.1 Dogs have lower visual acuity but are better at detecting motion.

Even when their vision is fully developed, the puppies will need to stand 20 feet from an object to see what a person would see at 75 feet. And although their field of vision is wider than that of humans, they will tend not to notice stationary objects, especially in their peripheral vision, until the objects move. If an object moves suddenly, it may startle the puppy or spark a chase response.

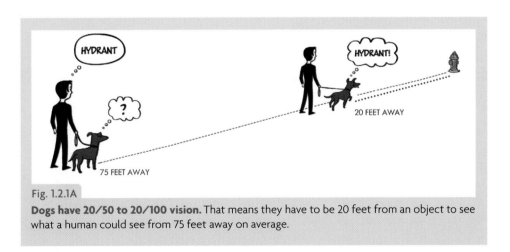

Fig. 1.2.1A

Dogs have 20/50 to 20/100 vision. That means they have to be 20 feet from an object to see what a human could see from 75 feet away on average.

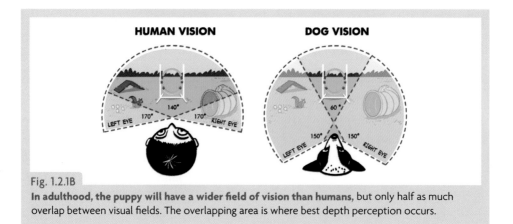

Fig. 1.2.1B

In adulthood, the puppy will have a wider field of vision than humans, but only half as much overlap between visual fields. The overlapping area is where best depth perception occurs.

1.2.2 Night vision.

There's a reflective layer of cells in the back of the dog's eye called the tapetum. It's the reason a dog's eyes seem to glow at night when you shine a light on them. The tapetum reflects light across the retina. Before the tapetum is fully developed, at 12 weeks of age, the retina has a purplish hue.

Dogs also have a high percentage of light-sensitive photoreceptors in their eyes. As a result, older puppies and adult dogs can see better at night compared to humans. In fact, they can see in four to five times less light than humans.

1.2.3 Are dogs color blind?

Contrary to older reports, dogs do see in color. It's just not as rich as color vision in humans. Humans have three different types of color receptors, called cones, and each cone type functions best at a different wavelength—red, green, or blue. All of the colors we humans see are produced by mixing red, green and blue light.

Dogs have two types of color receptors. One cone-type functions best in the violet-blue region and another type functions best in the yellow-green region. Consequently, dogs are a bit similar to humans who are red-green color blind.

We know that dogs have these receptors that transmit signals from the eye to the brain and that they also perceive differences in color because studies have been done in which dogs have been trained to pick the odd-colored circle out of a choice of three circles. To rule out hue or brightness as a distinguishing cue, the researches systematically tried patches of different brightness.

While we cannot determine exactly what the dog perceives the color to be, researchers think what we see as red, orange, yellow or green appears as different saturations of yellow to a dog, while blue-green, blue and violet appear as different saturations of bluish gray. So for dogs, if you want them to distinguish between colors, the best colors to use are blue and yellow.

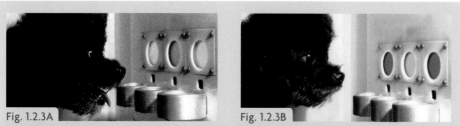

Fig. 1.2.3A   Fig. 1.2.3B

In discrimination studies, the dog is trained to indicate when he sees a circle that looks different from the other two. In this case he would pick the blue circle (Fig. 1.2.3A). Dogs can't distinguish between red and green, so in this trial the dog would not signal any difference because he can't see any (Fig. 1.2.3B). Photos courtesy of Gerald Jacobs, Professor of Psychology, University of California, Santa Barbara

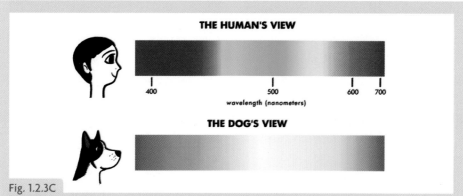

Fig. 1.2.3C

Dogs have two types of color photoreceptors while humans have three. As a result, dogs probably perceive the world in different saturations of yellow or bluish-gray.

Fig. 1.2.3D

These photos depict the colors that humans with normal color vision see versus what a dog is likely to see. Photo courtesy of Dr. Cynthia Cook of Veterinary Vision, Inc. Animal Eye Specialists (www.veterinaryvision.com)

1.3 The Transition Period (14 to 21 Days).

By 14 days, the eyes are open and the ears will open shortly, enabling the puppies to start recognizing and bonding with littermates and the humans and other pets around them. The development of these senses coincides with the ability to stand and then move around, so that by 21 days the puppies start playing with and exploring their environment.

1.3.1 What do puppies hear?

A puppy's vision and hearing systems are both incomplete at birth. The ear canals open at 12 to 14 days, and once the ears are open, puppies may startle when they hear sounds. They generally recover quickly though. Right from the start, the range of hearing is nearly twice that of humans; dogs can hear from 20 Hz to 35 kHz—well into the ultrasonic range.

Fig. 1.3.1A
These 23-day-old puppies can stand and walk now. By this age they can also see and hear and bond with other animals in their environment.

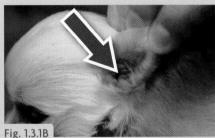

Fig. 1.3.1B
And at 23 days of age you can easily see their open ear canals.

1.3.2 As soon as puppies can hear we can start habituating them to new sounds.

As soon as puppies can hear, the breeder or caretaker should consider playing sound CDs so that the puppies can get accustomed to the type of sounds they will hear later on in life. This way they are less likely to become fearful of common sounds due to lack of early exposure. These sounds include: traffic, car doors slamming, fireworks, thunder, jack hammers, pots clanging, sirens, children among others. It's especially important to expose the puppies to CDs with these sounds if the breeder or caretaker lives in an environment in which they are not likely to hear these sounds otherwise. For instance, if she lives in the countryside, the puppies are not likely to be exposed to the sounds of loud traffic.

Fig. 1.3.2A

Recorded sounds such as those on the SoundsGood CDs (Legacy Canine; www.legacycanine.com) can be a great way to start getting young puppies accustomed to sounds they will hear later in life. Play the sound at a low volume and increase the volume once the puppies clearly show no reaction to the sound at the current volume (Figure 1.3.2A).

1.4 The Sensitive Period for Socialization: (Three Weeks to Three Months).

Once puppies can see and hear and get around well, they start interacting more with their littermates as well as their environment. This is when they are primed for bonding to other animals and individuals, for learning that objects, people, and environments are safe, and for learning what the body cues and signals of others mean. It is the sensitive period for socialization. It runs from roughly three weeks to three months of age and it is the most important socialization period in a dog's life. Puppies who do not get adequate socialization during this period tend to be fearful of unfamiliar people, or dogs, or sounds, or objects and environments. Most people mistakenly think that such dogs must have been abused early in life but their fear is most commonly a product of incomplete or inadequate socialization for the particular individual's needs. Since this golden period starts before puppies go to their final home it's important that the breeders or early caretakers start the process of providing the puppies with the positive experiences needed to adapt well to living with humans.

Fig. 1.4A
At 3.5 weeks of age, while the other puppies explore this puppy-safe play area, the one on the right hides and falls asleep against the back of the pen. He also trembles and is less willing to eat when unfamiliar people hold him. He is fearful. But once he's put back in his familiar whelping area, he is more comfortable so he explores and starts to eat again.

Fig. 1.4B
By 4.5 weeks, with frequent handling paired with food, and visits to new environments, this puppy is now relaxed when being held by unfamiliar people and more exploratory in various environments. In this photo we hold the clippers up to him to get him used to the sound of the clippers and the feel of its vibrations. His coat is likely to need trimming when he gets older and the experience will be more pleasant if he's not fearful.

1.4.1 Learning how to interact with other dogs.

During this socialization period puppies start learning how to interact with others and about the consequences of their interactions. For instance, they may learn that when mom raises her lip, it may be followed by a snap and a reprimand. So the pups learn to be mindful of her body language.

What they learn depends on the type of interactions they have. Just as individual children grow up with different parenting styles and sibling interaction that shape their overall behavior and personality, individual puppies and puppies from different litters are partly a product of the animals and humans they interact with.

Puppies may or may not learn to temper their play:

Fig. 1.4.1A   Fig. 1.4.1B   Fig. 1.4.1C

All of the puppies play roughly with the runt of the litter. All of the puppies in this litter play roughly with the runt of the litter. They grab her and shake her by the scruff. As they get older they may learn to temper their play if roughness causes play to stop or if it consistently causes the other puppy to snap intensely enough to make her message clear.

Fig. 1.4.1D

By week eight it's clear that some puppies playing with siblings can learn inappropriate play skills. The puppies in this litter play frequently but at about 6 weeks of age the larger puppy started playing too roughly and growling when playing with his siblings. This caused one of his siblings, the smaller puppy in this photo, to become overly aroused too and the two would fight for up to 5 seconds. Over a two week period the fights increased in intensity until they were occurring about 2-3x a day and in about 50% of observed play bouts. The foster caretaker started training alternate behaviors by just calling the puppies and getting their attention so they would not continue to practice being overly aroused.

Fig. 1.4.1E

Learning to respect personal space: By interacting with an adult dog, Jonesy, these puppies have learned that they need to be respectful of some dogs around food. Even the rowdy pup who also growls at the others over food has learned to back away when Jonesy's getting food out of the puzzle toy. This is an important lesson that is best to learn when young. If the rowdy puppy gets a lot of practice growling at other dogs for months and then finally gets growled at as an adolescent, instead of backing down, he may be so aroused that he escalates to physical aggression.

Fig. 1.4.1F

Learning from positive experiences: These puppies have had positive experiences with Jonesy and other dogs already. We've given them lots of treats when they have been around new dogs so that we can ensure their experiences have been positive. We've also rewarded calm sitting behavior when around other dogs. As a result, these puppies do not accidentally learn to be afraid of Jonesy or other dogs who reprimand them appropriately. They have specifically learned to give Jonesy space when he's around food.

" During the sensitive period for socialization (three weeks to three months of age) puppies start learning how to interact with others and about the consequences of their interactions. "

The puppies in this litter have been snapped at by their mom when they have chewed on her legs and tail. They have stopped their chewing temporarily but then gone back to bothering her 30 seconds later. However, with Jonesy, who roars like a lion over minor infractions even though he never bites, they remember their lesson, even a week later.

Fig. 1.4.1G

Fig. 1.4.1H

Fig. 1.4.1I

Fig. 1.4.1J

Jonesy has had a lasting effect on these puppies: In this scenario we placed two puppies on the other end of the grass so that we could take photos of them running to us. Because Jonesy has chosen to chew on a bone at the edge of the grass between them and us the puppies hesitate as if plotting what to do next. (Figure 1.4.1G,H) Then they sprint by giving Jonesy a wide berth. (Figure 1.4.1I) Notice this puppy's ears are back because she is a little fearful of what might happen if she gets too close. (Figure 1.4.1J)

Here's what the puppy looks like when she is running playfully. Note the forward ear position.

Fig. 1.4.1K

Lucy has had many positive experiences with dogs even before seven weeks of age: As a puppy, Lucy has interacted with a number of adult dogs owned by her breeder. Within her litter the puppies were getting in spats because they tended to play too rambunctiously. But upon first greeting with a dog that I brought when I visited, Lucy was well mannered. She walked up to him, a little tentatively to greet. She had never seen a dog with a smushed face. Once she greeted him she was completely relaxed and interested in interacting but not overly focused on him. Equally important, she was polite and did not try to jump all over him like she would with her mom and siblings.

Fig. 1.4.1L

1.4.2 Providing positive experiences with unfamiliar people of different sizes, genders, ethnicities.

Because dogs are frequently fearful of unfamiliar people, especially men, it is essential that they be exposed to many people starting before they go to their final homes. The breeder or early caretakers should invite guests to come interact with the puppies while providing treats and toys to ensure the puppies are having a positive experience. Interacting with only household humans is not enough.

Fig. 1.4.2A
These puppies were nervous at first when they were handled by visitors. They showed their anxiety by trembling when held or refusing to take treats and moving around and playing less when the visitors were around. They were also more fearful of men, a common occurrence with dogs and puppies. By six weeks of age, after having several visitors a week, they are now relaxed around most new visitors, including men.

Fig. 1.4.2B
It's important that visitors wear a variety of clothes. My Jack Russell Terrier, Jonesy, randomly barked at people wearing Ugg® boots for a year and he barked at one of my assistants because he didn't recognize her when she was wearing this hooded sweater. One of the puppies from the litter pictured here also reacted to this person's hood or her boots. He barked at her once while jumping back. Then he decided she was safe and approached to get treats.

To puppies and dogs who have never seen kids, children can look like little aliens. As puppies mature, children can also start looking more like toys or things they should chase because they scream and run and flail their arms like injured prey. If the breeder does not have or know children whom the puppies can interact with she should at least play sounds of children and babies from a sound CD such as SoundsGood CD (www. legacycanine.com). The new family should also be told that the puppy is lacking in this experience and that they should make a special effort to provide good interactions with children.

Fig. 1.4.2C

These puppies have never seen a child, but because they've been socialized to so many other things by seven weeks of age, they immediately accept this child as safe.

Fig. 1.4.2D

The child also knows how to feed them treats and this helps them to associate her with good experiences. Because these puppies have already been handled a lot, they let the child pick them up and remain relaxed regardless of the position in which she holds them.

1.4.3 Socializing puppies to other species.

Many puppies will live with cats or other animals at some time during their life or they may see animals of other species. It would be best if they could react calmly instead of barking, lunging or chasing these other animals.

Fig. 1.4.3A

Reward calm behavior when other animals are present: This puppy is learning to sit calmly in the presence of the cat. Not only do we want dogs to feel safe and unafraid around other animals, we also want them to behave calmly. So we should reward calm behavior. This puppy's entire litter is good with cats—at least those cats in two household settings. The puppies sometimes try to solicit play but are not overly rambunctious when the cats decline by walking away. Lucy's breeder has exposed her to cats too which should make it easier to train Lucy to be calm around any new cats she meets.

1.4.4 Learning to walk on different surfaces.

Probably everyone knows a dog who's afraid of walking on metal manhole covers in the street or grates on the sidewalk. Or dogs who won't step on wet grass to go potty. By exposing puppies to different surfaces when they are young we can greatly decrease the likelihood they will be afraid of walking on a variety of surfaces later in life. This exposure to different surfaces is something that can easily be started by the breeder-especially since the sense of touch is well developed, even at birth.

Fig. 1.4.4A

Fig. 1.4.4B

Walking on wood surfaces: This puppy is receiving treats for walking on a rough, raised wooden surface. Because of this she has no problem stepping onto the surface herself.

Fig. 1.4.4C   Fig. 1.4.4D   Fig. 1.4.4E

Walking on metal surfaces: These puppies find yummy treats on this metal surface and readily climb on. With repeated practice they will have no problems standing on a metal scale or metal table at the veterinary hospital. We are using small pieces of Natural Balance food roll, but we could also just use a portion of their regular meal during these exercises.

Standing on an exam table: This puppy has no fear of being on the metal examination table at the veterinary hospital. We give him treats to ensure that he has a positive experience. We're using baby food on a tongue depressor as our treat.

Fig. 1.4.4F   Fig. 1.4.4G   Fig. 1.4.4H

Climbing on an elevated surface: This puppy is learning to climb up on a low-lying ironing board which is about the same height as the riser between steps in a staircase. He feels confident enough to leap off. With this one obstacle, he's learning to navigate climbing and heights and is getting used to an ironing board which some dogs find scary. This seems like a small feat; however, my Jack Russell Terrier, Jonesy, although fearless with heights, was fearful of ironing boards for many months after I adopted him.

Fig. 1.4.4I   Fig. 1.4.4J

Balancing on wobbly objects: This puppy is learning to stand and balance on wobbly objects. This is great for building confidence as well as improving athletic ability.

Fig. 1.4.4K

Skateboards and other objects with wheels: It's not unusual for dogs to fear items with wheels like skateboards and strollers. This puppy is learning to associate the skateboard with good experiences. Next we need to start moving the skateboard around so that it makes noise while keeping the puppy in a happy state either on the skateboard or standing in sight of it. Other rolling items to work with include strollers, shopping carts, and luggage with wheels.

Fig. 1.4.4L

Exposure to water and wet grass: The weather during the first eight weeks of these puppies' lives has been warm and dry. As a result, they haven't had any exposure to rain, cold, or wet grass. The best simulation we have is a little infant pool with water and fake grass. This will help accustom them to the feel so that they don't grow up to be sissies who can't go out to potty when the weather is rainy and the yard is wet. You can use wet sod or mud instead of fake grass.

Fig. 1.4.4M

Exposure to frost or snow: These Corgi puppies live in Alaska so they are receiving exposure to the cold early on. They run on the frost and play in the cold like it's normal for them, because it is.

Imagine what housetraining would look like if these guys didn't like going outside in the cold weather!

Fig. 1.4.4N

Preparing puppies for a bath: At some point the puppies will need a bath. We can prepare by giving them treats while they are in a tub-like setting.

1.4.5 Introducing puppies to other man-made objects and sounds.

Most people never appreciate the every-day sounds and sights that might be frightening to a pet or even a person raised in a completely different environment. But once you have a dog who missed out on key environmental experience when young it can be overwhelming to deal with all of the objects they fear.

Fig. 1.4.5A

Dogs must learn that regular everyday objects are safe. Jonesy, the Jack Russell Terrier that I adopted at eight months of age, poses with some of the objects he used to be afraid of but is OK with now. When walking down a typical city street he would bark at or tremble and shy away from about two to three objects per block—garbage cans, sidewalk signs, murals of dogs, skateboards, metal pipe sticking out of the wall. The list goes on. He was fearful because he'd been raised in a rural environment.

Fig. 1.4.5B

Brooms and cleaning equipment: These well-socialized pups have no fear of this new object, a broom.

Fig. 1.4.5C

Brooms and cleaning equipment: To Jonesy however, the broom coming towards him is as scary as a knife.

Fig. 1.4.5D

Plastic bags: Another common item that startles dogs is plastic bags that float around in the wind. To these puppies it's just another item littering their environment.

Fig. 1.4.5E

Many dogs are afraid of vacuum cleaners and similar objects. They stay away or bark and lunge at the objects—sometimes even while wagging their tails. This can make cleaning the house an extra chore. Here we turn the vacuum on but start with it far away while giving the puppies treats. If they won't take treats, then the vacuum is too close or too loud.

Fig. 1.4.5F

Fig. 1.4.5G

When the puppies are completely comfortable with the loudness and distance of the vacuum cleaner it can be moved closer.

1.4.6 Training them to love crates and car rides.

It's easy to train puppies to ride in a crate or car especially when they are under 8 weeks of age, and it's important too. Once the puppy is adopted she will generally need to ride in a car to her new home. The safest seat for puppies in a car is in a crate. If the puppy is not already used to these things then the trip to her new home can be quite traumatic.

To train young puppies to enjoy crates and car rides, just place them in a crate with treats for short periods and let them out when they are quiet. For car rides, just take them for multiple short car rides to places where they have good experiences (such as back to their familiar home) and give treats too. Barely any effort is required for most puppies at this young age.

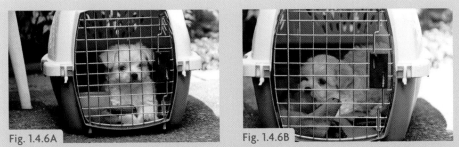

Fig. 1.4.6A   Fig. 1.4.6B

These puppies have been taken on a number of car rides starting at three weeks of age. They have also been individually crated and separated from each other starting at six weeks of age. By eight weeks of age most can make it through the night without whining.

Chapter 2

Why Start Training So Soon?

Shortly after I got Lucy, when she was well on her way to being happy and well-behaved, I called my dad and told him I had his new dog. Remembering how he had started with our first two dogs 30 and 25 years ago, he asked, "Should I get her a choke chain? And a big bowl?" Boy! Have times changed. »

Several decades ago I wouldn't have batted an eye. Back when I started, training was mostly all force-based and our rewards were just praise. We put dogs on choke chains or pinch collars and yanked them when they did things wrong. We assumed that they knew exactly what we wanted and were being stubborn or willful if they weren't well-behaved.

Now that I knew about science-based training methods, I almost gasped. At this point in our training Lucy was already sitting politely for everything she wanted and coming when called. The thought of giving this sweet, innocent pup a correction of any sort would be like spanking an infant for putting something in her mouth!

When I first started training, all dog training was force-based. It focused on correcting unwanted behavior using a choke chain or pinch collar. Times have changed and now I could not imagine having either product on Lucy, especially at just eight weeks of age when she was just learning the rules and had already learned to be so well-behaved.

Fig. 2A

Realistically, I don't think my dad was planning on giving her a choke chain correction. Even my traditional Chinese dad had learned that training is different now and had lamented at how mean he'd been with our other dogs. He understood the importance of rewarding desired behavior with food and other rewards. But his understanding was very basic and things had changed much more than he knew.

The training of this pup was going to be way different from anything he remembered—and very different from what most people do.

2.1 Is It Safe to Start So Soon?

One practice that has changed in the last 20 years is the age at which we start training and socializing pups. You may have heard that you should wait until your puppy has gotten his shots to socialize him or until he's six months of age until you train him. Well, partly due to Ian Dunbar and his movement to make puppy socialization classes the norm, it's now more widely known that puppies need positive experiences with many people, pets and places, usually starting by at least eight weeks of age. That's because these early weeks are the prime time for puppies to form bonds with other individuals and learn to recognize other animals and environments as being safe. (More about this in chapter 6.)

If you omit this structured early learning and wait too long, as the puppy matures he may become fearful of new things. As a default behavior when he's afraid, he may defend himself by barking, growling at and later biting these scary stimuli.

What we have especially learned in the past few years is that the benefits of this socialization far outweigh the risks of catching any infectious disease, as long as proper precautions are taken to protect the puppy. For instance, we recommend you walk your puppy in neighborhoods where most dogs are vaccinated and stay away from parks (especially dog parks) and other areas frequented by dogs of unknown vaccination status.

The American Veterinary Society of Animal Behavior Position Statement on Puppy Socialization recommends that puppies be given many positive experiences with various people, places and environments starting well before 12 weeks of age. (To download this position statement as well as a roundtable discussion on the topic go to www. AVSABonline.org).

Fig. 2.1A

2.2 Won't We Break the Puppy's Spirit?

In the past, when training was primarily based on using a variety of corrections (choke chain, pinch collar, forcing puppies onto their sides or backs, spray bottles, cans that make noise, electronic shock collars) to punish unwanted behaviors, puppies crumbled under the pressure and shut down. In fact, I remember training our second childhood puppy to walk on a leash by just hooking him on and letting him scream until he started walking, and thinking that this is how you were supposed to do it. He just had to buck up! Because this type of harsh training early in life could produce a variety of possible future negative effects, the trainers who used these techniques developed the idea that you couldn't train puppies until they were old enough to handle "tough" training without being "ruined."

Techniques we use now in early learning are similar to those used for kids. We focus primarily on controlling the environment and rewarding desirable behaviors to build confidence. Puppies aren't "ruined" or even scared by these techniques. We also make sure the puppy does not receive rewards for unwanted behavior.

Some aversive-based trainers do still use negatives to train puppies. In fact, aversive-based trainers even use shock collars at low levels to train puppies by removing the low-level zapping when the puppy does what they want. The shock is relatively low,

The approach we use now in training puppies is similar to the approach we use for kids. We focus primarily on controlling the environment in order to prevent unwanted behaviors from occurring and we focus on rewarding the behaviors we want. We also make sure we avoid rewarding unwanted behaviors.

Fig. 2.2A

but it is enough to stop the pup in his tracks and make him want to immediately figure out how to turn it off, even if he was interested in doing something else.

While such training may seem fine to someone who's never experienced anything else, to those who are careful readers of canine body language and encourage dogs to solve problems, we often see subtle or even major negative effects down the road. A puppy with a confident personality may be just fine with this type of training, except he may just be less willing to try new things or learn new behaviors without precise guidance—since creativity and many new behaviors earn him low-level shocks. A softer, more sensitive or incompletely socialized puppy may have more serious fear-based consequences when aversive methods are used.

As a result, AVSAB, as well as board-certified veterinary behaviorists (www. dACVB.org or www.AVSABonline.org) and certified applied animal behaviorists in general (www.animalbehaviorsociety.org), recommend positive-based methods for all dogs, especially puppies. They advise against coercion-based training as a first line of training.

2.3 How Will the Puppy Learn Right From Wrong?

Animals, including puppies, perform behaviors that are reinforced even when the reward is unintentional. So to train polite behavior we will focus on:

- **Controlling the environment** so that the puppy doesn't have a chance to practice unwanted behaviors (chewing your shoes, climbing on chairs, raiding the trash).

- **Removing reinforcers**—attention, petting, tug, treats or play—for unwanted behaviors.

- **Rewarding only the desirable behaviors** instead, such as sitting to greet instead of jumping or focusing on you instead of harassing your adult dog. We'll use all motivators to our advantage.

If this sounds a lot like how you would raise a child, it's not a coincidence. The laws that govern learning and behavior in dogs also guide behavior in cats, horses, goats, giraffes and all other animals, including children.

2.4 Is It Okay to Wait a Week or More for the Puppy to Settle in Before Starting the Training?

As soon as the pup enters the house, he begins to learn and form habits. You can't stop this from happening. Whether or not you're aware of it, every interaction you have with the puppy is a learning session. The puppy's either learning behaviors you consider naughty or he's learning to be polite, happy and well-behaved.

The humans in the household are developing habits, too. They may be learning to unconsciously reward behaviors that can become a bigger problem later on, and the humans may have problems changing their patterns of interaction with the pup. In general, it's best to develop good habits right away in both human and pet, rather than teaching the puppy undesirable habits you will later need to fix. But don't worry, the training is fun. And systematically rewarding good behavior is a wonderful way to bond with your pup and develop a happy dog. If you wait a few weeks and suddenly start training, your training technique will need to be five times better, because your dog will have to unlearn as well as learn. Plus your puppy will be more coordinated and better able to perform problem behaviors, just the way toddlers become more challenging as soon as they can walk.

Fig. 2.4A   Fig. 2.4B   Fig. 2.4C   Fig. 2.4D

Start handling exercise early while the puppy is still small and easy to physically position and hold (Figures 2.4A). This 12-week-old puppy is friendly to people. If you try to examine her mouth or handle her feet she already growls, tries to bite, and struggles violently (Figures 2.4B,C,D) Imagine how she will be at the veterinary hospital or for basic care and grooming as an adult! With each week the behavior may become more difficult for owners to fix. Puppies change quickly during their early weeks. So by waiting even a week or two to start training and handling exercises you may end up needing to work way harder to fix problems.

Fig. 2.4E   Fig. 2.4F   Fig. 2.4G

INCORRECT: Start training before bad habits form: Figure 2.4 E,F,G: Chewing on objects, nipping on arms, raiding the garbage, jumping on people and climbing on furniture— these are behaviors that puppies will naturally perform. Without a prevention plan in place, the behaviors may become well established which makes them more challenging to change. Additionally, as the puppy matures, the damage from these behaviors may increase. It's best to form desired habits from the start by beginning your puppy's training on day 1.

2.5 Here's a Reason to Start Early.

Training your pup is about setting clear rules and guidelines, and communicating them by rewarding the desired behaviors exactly as they occur and removing rewards for the undesired behaviors. While our habit is to use human words, in truth what animals and puppies care about is your body language and the actual consequences of their actions. That means humans have to be aware of their every movement around a pet, because their movement is what conveys their wishes.

Consequently, training is a skill that must be practiced, like playing tennis, dancing or playing the piano. Little variations in how you move and the timing of the rewards make a big difference in whether you can communicate your intentions to the pet. When puppies are really young, they are slower and less coordinated than adults. As a result, it's easier for you to get the reward to them while they are still performing the desired behavior and before they go on to a different behavior. So by starting young, you'll be able to get away with less precise timing and skill on your part.

Chapter 3

Preparing for the Puppy

Before you bring the puppy home, you'll first want to get a few vital supplies. »

3.1 What You Need.

Fig. 3.1A

Crate/pooch palace: All puppies need a safe, comfortable place to sleep, both at night and during the day, and when you take trips. Get a crate or travel kennel that will fit your dog as an adult. If he will be in the crate for extended amounts of time when he's full grown, it should be large enough for an adult-sized version of him to stand with several inches of clearance and to turn around and stretch out.

Fig. 3.1B

Bed outside the crate: Your pup also needs a comfortable bed or rug as a resting spot in each room where he spends a significant amount of time.

Fig. 3.1C

Baby gate: A baby gate works well now, and even in the future when you have guests, to keep the dog confined while still having visual access.

Fig. 3.1D

Cover trash cans: Just the way you baby proof a house when you have kids you should also puppy-proof the house when you get a puppy. That means eliminating the opportunity for them to raid the trash can by placing trash cans within cabinets, elevated, or in cans with lids.

Fig. 3.1E

Fig. 3.1F

Toys: Make sure you have a variety of toys and a place to store them, so your puppy has access to some of them, but not all at once. Puppies love to switch between toys rather then choosing just one and sticking with it.

Commercial dog food: Use a food labeled as complete and balanced for puppies or for all stages of life, as tested by AAFCO feeding trials. My preference is one with kibble the size of a bite-size treat. Big dogs need bigger kibble. Some people prefer to home-prepare their puppy's meals. If you choose this, you should use recipes shown to be balanced by a veterinarian who is board-certified in nutrition (www.acvn.org). The vast majority of recipes in many of the highly popular books, even those written by veterinarians (who are not nutritionists) have been shown to be inadequate and unbalanced. There are some veterinary nutritionist services that provide custom recipes to owners (www.balanceIT.com and www.petDIETS.com).

Fig. 3.1G

Fig. 3.1H

Treats: Use your puppy's regular allotment of kibble for most of the training. Use small, bite-size treats for more challenging situations (Fig. 3.1G). Sometimes you can use a different brand of dog food kibble as treats. For instance here's a kibble (Fig. 3.1H) designed for ease of chewing by Bulldogs or Boxers. This kibble serves as fun-shaped treats for dogs on other diets. My dogs like them as much as any other dry dog treat. I generally break each of these kibble into 2-3 pieces.

Fig. 3.1I

Fig. 3.1J

Food reward bag: You'll want food rewards close by, so that you're always ready to reward good behavior as it happens, rather than being 5 to 10 seconds late. I like bags that snap open and close, rather than ones that require drawstrings or Velcro. The Terry Ryan bait bag made by Premier Pet products is my favorite. It's best to have a treat bag rather than sticking food in your pockets, because it will be important to be able to get the treats quickly and sometimes that doesn't happen when the food is stored in a pocket.

Fig. 3.1K

Leash and collar: Use a snap or buckle collar, or a harness that snaps in the front for easy guiding (such as the EasyWalk Harness by Premier Pet products or SENSE-ation harness). I prefer a hands-free leash you tie around your waist so that you don't give unintended signals when you hold the leash in your hand. My favorite is the Buddy System (www.buddysys.com).

Fig. 3.1L

Grooming tools: You'll also need various grooming supplies such as brushes, nail trimmers and a toothbrush and dog toothpaste for dental care.

Fig. 3.1M

Appointment with your veterinarian: All puppies should be examined within three days of adoption. While some people are against vaccinations and can sometimes get away without vaccinating their dog if the canine population where they live is largely vaccinated, foregoing vaccinations carries serious risks. As a rule, all puppies should be vaccinated at 6 to 8 weeks, 9 to 11 weeks and 12 to 14 weeks (according to the AAHA Guidelines for pet dogs). After that, it's a booster at one year and then every three years, but it depends on the type of vaccine given and your dog's risk. It's best to consult your veterinarian, who will be up to date on current recommendations and risk in your area. Instead of automatically giving vaccine boosters, you can have a titer taken and if immunity is high, there's no need for vaccination.

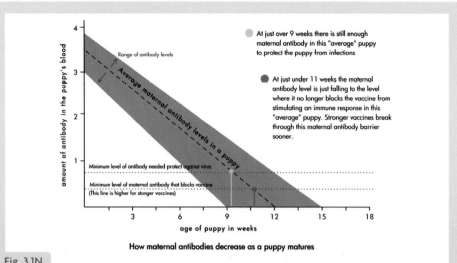

Fig. 3.1N

Why multiple vaccinations? Why multiple vaccinations in puppies? Our current vaccines are excellent at stimulating immunity in older puppies in just one or two shots. However, puppies who nursed on their mother's milk have maternal antibodies in their blood that block the immune system from responding to these vaccines. These circulating maternal antibodies protect them from bacterial and viral assault while their immune system is maturing. They also prevent the puppy's immune system from becoming activated by vaccines. As the puppy ages, the maternal antibody levels decline. By as early as 6 weeks, 25% of puppies have a strong immune response to vaccinations, and by 14 to 16 weeks of age the maternal antibodies have fallen enough to allow a full immune response in 90% of puppies. Veterinarians administer vaccines starting around 6 to 8 weeks of age to increase the likelihood that as the maternal antibodies are falling, the lower levels don't leave the puppy exposed to disease but instead, the immune system is activated.

3.2 One Surprise Item You Do *Not* Need and What to Use in Its Place.

3.2.1 Avoid using a food bowl.

Instead of eating out of a food bowl your puppy will at first be earning all his food from you directly as rewards for good behavior. We do this because for the fastest training we need to use all motivators to our advantage. That means you use every morsel of food as a reward, rather than wasting it by giving it to him for free.

Fig. 3.2.1A

INCORRECT: No food bowl: Avoid feeding your puppy out of a food bowl. He'll be earning all food through training or in a food toy. There are a variety of food dispensing toys on the market.

3.2.2 Use a food puzzle instead.

Even if you aren't using your puppy's food to build your bond, throwing his food into a bowl is like buying T.V. dinners for your kids instead of taking time to cook something healthy. It's best to at least put the puppy's food in a food toy to keep your puppy engaged and solving problems. That way his brain can develop while he's burning off energy and keeping himself out of trouble.

Fig. 3.2.2A   Fig. 3.2.2B

Use food toys if you don't have time to feed during training sessions. There are a variety of food-dispensing toys on the market, such as the Egg-Cersizer® by Premier Pet Products (Figure 3.2.2A) and the Bob-A-Lot® by StarMark Pet Products (Figure 3.2.2B). The puppy pushes these toys around causing kibble to fall out.

Fig. 3.2.2C

Fig. 3.2.2D

One popular food toy is a Kong®. To train the puppy to eat out of this toy, mix her dry kibble with some canned food to help hold the kibble together. Then stuff the Kong® with this mixture. (Figures 3.2.2C,D).

Fig. 3.2.2E

Fig. 3.2.2F

Here's how to prepare a more challenging Kong® toy treat. To increase the challenge of getting the food out of the Kong®, make a Kong® toy food popsicle. Plug the bottom of the Kong toy with peanut butter, canned cheese, or canned food (Figure 3.2.2E). Then fill the Kong® toy with your puppy's regular kibble or kibble mixed with canned food (Figure 3.2.2F).

Fig. 3.2.2G

Fig. 3.2.2H

Next place the Kong® toy in a container so it stands upright and fill it with water (Figure 3.2.2G). Then place it in the freezer (Figure 3.2.2H). You can fill and store a bunch at a time to use as needed. My dogs take about 30 minutes to work their way through this. It's like getting a bone to chew at each meal.

Chapter 4

A Foolproof Potty Training Program

One of the most trying tasks associated with having a puppy is potty training. »

Some people think potty training is as easy as just keeping the pup on a regular eating, drinking and potty-outing schedule where she is taken out every several hours. Or they think the pup will be completely housetrained in just a week or two. For some precocious pups this might be so; however, many puppies taken through such a lax, abbreviated potty protocol remain only partially housetrained, or they have potty accidents for months. These little Rovers learn that pottying outside is good, but they do not understand that inside is out of bounds. In fact, they may even come inside after an extensive play or exercise period and relieve themselves on your expensive carpet.

That's because potty training is not only about training where to go. It is also about making it clear that other places are inappropriate, until pottying only in the right locations becomes
a habit.

Does this seem odd to you? The same rules apply in our human world. For instance, in Paris public restrooms abound. There's easy access and they are clean. However, men prefer to randomly urinate in public on the walls. To help train men that it's inappropriate to urinate in public, the city has installed "pee walls" that cause the urine to splash on their feet. They have officers assigned to what they call a Bad Behavior Brigade who ticket public pee-ers. As the Wall Street Journal reports, they are saying non non to oui oui and making it difficult for men to potty in the wrong locations, in hopes that the men will form a habit of only going in the right places.

In this section I'll show you a foolproof potty training plan that works even for breeds known to be difficult to housetrain. All you have to do is follow it and you'll experience success.

" Potty training is more than just taking your puppy out every few hours. It requires you control the puppy's environment and schedule so he does not have the chance to have accidents."

Potty Training Tips

Prevention Is the Key

The key to potty training is taking your young puppy out frequently (on average every two hours for an eight-week-old puppy) and never giving her the opportunity to have a potty accident. That means at least eight trips a day!

To avoid giving your pup the opportunity to potty inside, when she's in the house she should always either be

- **in her crate**
- **in a puppy-safe and potty-safe playpen** with a potty area that contains a preferred potty surface (such as fake grass or pee pads)
- **attached to you by a leash** so she can't wander off to potty in the house
- **or under your direct supervision** in an enclosed area. Direct supervision means you are looking at her at all times. The minute you turn away, she'll have a potty accident.

Stick to this plan for a month straight and she'll reliably develop the habit of going outside and holding it inside. Then continue keeping a close eye on her for another couple of months, especially when you take her on outings to other people's homes, before declaring her completely potty trained.

4.1 Potty Training Starts With Learning To Love And Sleep In A Crate (Or Other Small, Enclosed Area).

The goal of crate training is that your puppy learns to love resting in her crate.

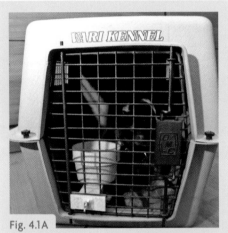

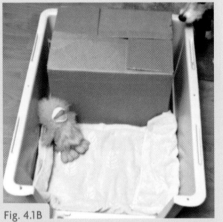

Fig. 4.1A

Crate: Your puppy should sleep in her crate at night and take naps in it during the day. To train her to love her crate, you can make it comfortable with a blanket and place treats inside at random times. Then give her toys and pet her when she's in it before you close the door. The ultimate goal of crate training is that she goes into the crate on her own or when you give her a verbal cue, rather than needing to be shoved or coaxed in. And once she's in, she remains calm, relaxed and quiet. (If you have problems with this, download the crate training handout at www.drsophiayin.com.)

Fig. 4.1B

Crate size: The crate should be big enough for the puppy to lie down and turn around but not big enough for a separate potty area. You can make the crate smaller by placing a box in it and, as the puppy grows, enlarge the crate by using a smaller box.

" The goal of crate training is that your puppy learns to love resting in her crate. "

4.1.1 Crates and whining.

Most puppies whine the first time they are crated. They aren't used to having restricted access to their family. It's important that puppies learn that being separated or confined is okay, and that they learn it NOW or you may end up with a puppy who develops full blown anxiety whenever she is left alone in a room or behind a baby gate or at home or whenever she can't go where she wants - even if she's restricted just by leash.

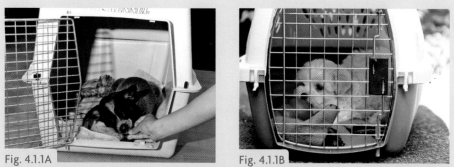

Fig. 4.1.1A   Fig. 4.1.1B

Provide puppies with something positive while they are in their crates. You can place treats and some of your puppy's meal in the crate every time you put her in, so that she associates being in the crate with positive experiences. You can even place a portion of her meal in a Kong® toy. Mix a little canned food with kibble so she has to work to get the food out of the toy. It's best if the treats/toys keep her engaged long enough so that she stays clam and feels relaxed when alone.

If you are diligent about the crate training early on, the whining should stop within a week. If you reward your puppy by letting her out when she whines, the whining could develop into serious anxiety or barrier frustration that prevents you from being able to leave your dog alone in another room or alone in the house.

Tips for Preventing and Dealing with Whining Puppies

- Avoid letting puppies out of their crates when they are barking or whining, or you'll reward the barking/whining behavior and it will get worse. Instead, wait until they are quiet to let them out.

- You can reward your puppy for quiet behavior by tossing treats into her crate when she's quiet or opening the door and giving her attention when she's quiet.

- Be sure to put treats and some of your puppy's meal in the crate every time you put her in, so that she associates being in the crate with positive experiences (Figure 4.1.1A). You can even place a portion of her meal in a Kong® toy. Mix a little canned food with kibble so she has to work to get the food out (Figure 4.1.1B). It's best if the food toy keeps her engaged long enough so she stays calm and relaxed when alone.

- If you are unsure whether the amount of whining is normal, consult an animal behavior specialist immediately (www.avsabonline.org, www.dacvb.org or www.animalbehaviorsociety.org) before the whining develops into an expensive and noisy problem.

- Some exceptional breeders train their puppies to love sleeping in a crate alone even before they adopt them out. If possible, see if your breeder will start the crate training before you pick your puppy up to take her home.

4.2 Potty Training Requires a Regular Schedule and Getting Puppy to Her Potty Spot Quickly.

Fig. 4.2A

First thing in the morning: When you let your pup out of her crate, rush her to her potty spot before she has a chance to squat and pee. If you're not sure that she can hold it long enough to make it outside, carry her out.

Fig. 4.2B

Walk briskly or run her to her potty spot: If you take her out without a leash, walk briskly or run down the hall so she doesn't have a chance to stop. She may have to be on leash so she doesn't have a chance to stop. Even a one-second stop will give her an opportunity to squat and potty inside. That means if you have stairs, it's best to carry her, since her hesitation right before the first stair is enough to allow her to squat and pee.

Note: Avoid picking your puppy up every time you want to take her outside to go potty. It may hinder her ability to learn to walk to the appropriate potty spot on her own.

Fig. 4.2C

Stand around until she potties: Once outside, keep her on a leash so she can't wander and get distracted, or alternatively place her in a small confined area outside. Stand silently until she potties. When she does, praise, pet her or give her a treat as she's finishing. Just be careful you don't distract her from finishing. If after five minutes she doesn't potty, put her in her crate for 15 minutes and then try again. Repeat this 20-minute procedure until she potties outside. After she has pottied, you can play with her.

Note: This can be tedious at first. Consider listening to music or a book on tape while you wait, and also having a timer so you don't get impatient for the five minutes outside. If your puppy doesn't potty the first time, remember to take her back out for a second try after 15 minutes in her crate.

4.2.1 How often should you take her out?

Fig. 4.2.1A

Start with every two hours for an eight-week-old puppy. Eight-week-old puppies can be crated for up to two hours during the day and through the entire night when they are sleeping. In general, during the day, puppies can be crated the same number of hours as their age in months. For example, a three-month-old puppy can be crated three hours at a time, if she hasn't had a large drink of water just before going into her crate.

Fig. 4.2.1B

Take her out after a nap: In addition to the two-hour rule, take the puppy out whenever she wakes up from sleeping or first comes out of her crate or playpen.

Fig. 4.2.1C

Take her out to potty after a play session: If she doesn't go potty, you can put her in her crate for 15 to 30 minutes and then take her out again.

Fig. 4.2.1D

Take her out when her body language says she's searching for a spot to pee: Signs that they are about to potty may be subtle. Typically they start sniffing the ground, circle, or wander away.

Fig. 4.2.1E

After a drink: Take her out to potty 10 to 20 minutes after she's had a drink of water. Remove her water about an hour before you take her out for her last potty trip of the day, so she can go through the night without pottying. She should be able to make it through the night for seven to eight hours.

Fig. 4.2.1F

Learn from your mistakes: Puppies have to potty seemingly a million times a day. Learn to predict when your puppy will need to go, and expect to have accidents. Each time she has an accident, you should learn from the experience and avoid making the same mistake again. Potty training is about establishing a habit of going to a potty spot whenever the dog has to go potty and never giving her the opportunity to have an accident inside.

4.2.2 Adding the cue to go potty.

When you can reliably predict when she is about to potty, you can add a cue word. Say "go potty" in a clear, encouraging voice just once, right before you think she will squat. If you can reliably say it within a couple of seconds before she has to squat, she will come to learn that "go potty" means she should do #1 or #2. Avoid saying the cue over and over, or it will just become noise to her.

4.3 Potty Training Requires Constant Supervision.

Until she's reliable, the puppy must be directly supervised or attached to you with a hands-free leash or near you on leash or resting in a playpen. Alternatively, she can be outside in a potty-safe and puppy-safe area. This may help her learn to potty when you are not outside to watch her. But avoid leaving her outside unsupervised for hours at a time. Also realize that young puppies are less able to withstand warm and cold temperatures.

Fig. 4.3A

Lucy is attached to me by a leash: This way she's always nearby, even when I'm moving from place to place. She's less likely to have a potty accident if she's right next to me because she's always in my sight and I can rush her outside. She's also less likely to get into trouble—chew inappropriate objects, climb on furniture, bother the other dog—because she's under my direct control and supervision.

Fig. 4.3B

Here she's attached by leash to furniture near me: From this position I can easily reward her for sitting or lying down quietly, and see that she's not wandering away to potty or chew an inappropriate object.

Fig. 4.3C

Make sure your pup has plenty of toys to keep her entertained: Wherever she's stationed, she should have lots of toys to chew on. If she grabs inappropriate items, such as your shoes or paper, remove them from her mouth and out of her range and place one of her puppy-approved items in her mouth. Similar to a two-year-old child, you'll have to repeat this toy trade many times for her to get the idea.

Fig. 4.3D

Make sure she has things to chew on: Here Lucy's chewing on a puppy-safe chew toy—a bully stick. An assortment of toys is essential for a developing puppy mind. When Lucy gets down to a final piece that's small enough to swallow whole but large enough to get stuck in her esophagus, stomach or intestines, I'll take the chew toy away.

Fig. 4.3E

Playpen: An alternative to crating when you're gone for longer periods of time is a puppy-safe playpen. It has her rug, water, toys and a potty spot covered with pee pads. Hopefully, she'll choose to potty on the pads if she can't wait to go outside. The goal with a playpen is that the puppy develops a substrate preference; she'll prefer to keep her bed clean and potty on the surface that is different from her bed.

Lucy's already used to pottying on artificial grass in the yard, so an indoor grass potty system might be a good substrate to use in her playpen.

Fig. 4.3F

What happens without eagle-eye supervision? Here's what happened when I let Lucy wander off leash for 20 seconds. Before this accident, she'd had no accidents for the first three days. On the fourth day I let her wander around off leash in a room with me three times. She had accidents two of those times, even though she had pottied outside five minutes earlier and was only out of my gaze for about 30 seconds. You can't keep your eye on a puppy every instant, unless the puppy is attached to you. All other times the puppy should be in her crate, in a playpen, tethered near you, or in a location where it's okay to go potty.

Fig. 4.3G

Outside in a potty-safe, puppy-safe yard: This will give her practice being independent and may help get her used to pottying in your absence outside. Make sure there are plenty of appropriate toys in the yard. Avoid leaving her unsupervised for long periods of time, especially in hot or cold weather. During her first week, Lucy spent 15 to 20 minutes at a time on her own outside in a fenced-in yard.

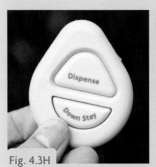
Fig. 4.3H

Fig. 4.3I

Fig. 4.3J

If you want, you can spy on your puppy and if you see her potty outside, you can reward her remotely with a Treat&Train or MannersMinder remote-controlled kibble and treat dispenser. First train her that treats come out of the machine. You control the release of treats by pressing the dispense button on a remote control (Fig 4.3 H). Then, put the machine outside with her and watch her from inside. When you see her potty outside, dispense treats as a reward. Here's an example with an older dog. (Fig 4.3I and Fig 4.3J) www.MannersMinder.net

4.4 What Happens When There's an Accident?

Fig. 4.4A

Interrupt your puppy: Try to interrupt her by making a sharp, guttural "ah". Don't yell or punish her. This can just teach her to avoid pottying in front of you or to be afraid of you. Don't even use "ah" if it scares her. Instead, whisk your puppy up.

Fig. 4.4B

Get her outside: Rush outside as quickly as possible!

Fig. 4.4C

Reward good behavior: Set her down in an appropriate potty spot and reward her with something she likes when she potties. After she has pottied you can play with her. Then vow to watch her more carefully next time.

Fig. 4.4D

Clean up: Clean the accident by sopping it up with a rag or a paper towel. Then soak the carpet or wipe the floor with an enzymatic cleaner so the area does not smell like pee or poop to your puppy. Examples of two good products are Petastic® and Anti-Icky Poo® (by MisterMax™).

4.5 What to do with Little Dogs or Puppies Who Dislike Going Outside to Potty in Cold Weather.

Some dogs dislike going outside in cold or wet weather, which can make potty training a challenge. This is where it really would have been useful if the breeder or early caretaker had provided the puppies with short positive exposures in cold or wet weather and wet grass or muddy surfaces before you took your puppy home. You can work on training your puppy to be more tolerant of the harsher environments by taking her out into situations that she can still tolerate and play in these environments. Alternatively, you can train her to potty inside on an indoor potty system.

Fig. 4.5A

Using an indoor potty system: One way to train puppies to use an indoor potty system such as this fake grass system is to leave them in an exercise pen in which one portion contains the bed and the other portion contains the potty system. Make sure that there's a clear difference between the soft resting surface of the bed and the potty surface. Puppies will tend to potty on the surface that is different from their bed.

Potty Training Tips

Potty training is about making it easy for the dog to potty outside and never providing an opportunity for her to go inside. If you can do this for a month, your puppy will have an established habit.

- Remember, the puppy doesn't understand that pottying in the house is wrong, any more than an infant understands that pooping in their diapers is gross. So don't scold the pup for your mistake. (You should have been watching.) Doing so is likely to teach the pup only to avoid pottying in your presence, and instead to have potty accidents behind your back.

- Even though puppies will try to keep their sleeping area and den area clean, if they are confined too long or have had too much water before being placed in their crate, they will still have accidents in the crate.

- If your puppy has an accident, just calmly clean it up and then figure out where you went wrong. Was she unsupervised? Did you miss her cues? Was she wandering freely? Then try to avoid making the same mistake again.

In her first week with me, Lucy only had two potty accidents. In both cases, they occurred when I got sloppy with the schedule and wasn't supervising her well.

Chapter 5

Dr. Sophia Yin's Learn to Earn Program for Puppies

When I first saw Lucy on a visit to her breeder, I was immediately happy with what I saw. The puppies were all outgoing and energetic and interested in interacting with and following me. At seven weeks of age, they were also extremely mature, active and coordinated compared to the average litter of puppies. They could sprint after their mom around the two-acre field in the hopes of a chance to nurse. And after doing a lap or two, they played constantly for the next half hour. Sometimes they played too roughly—enough to get into little spats. It was a good indicator that it was almost time for them to be separated into homes, rather than practicing too much overly rough behavior.

Fig. 5.1A

At seven weeks Lucy and her littermates were athletic, energetic and playing so roughly that they repeatedly got into little spats. This was a good indicator that it was almost time for them to be separated into homes where individuals could be provided with supervised interactions with friendly, well-mannered, adult dogs. That way they could learn to play in a more controlled manner.

When I got Lucy home, she immediately proved herself adorable. Play and attention were her goals, but the problem was that she focused most of her energy on climbing and jumping and nipping on arms. Cute at this age, but my first thought was, "Uh oh! Imagine her in a couple of weeks and a little larger, knocking my senior citizen parents down or scratching open my mom's diabetic skin." I saw broken hips and nip-induced infections in my parents' future. I needed to get her trained to sit politely to get what she wanted, and to play with appropriate toys rather than jumping and nipping. Luckily, I had just the plan for accelerated training: my version of the Learn to Earn program (see a video overview at www.drsophiayin.com on the Videos page).

5.1 The Program Basics.

The Learn to Earn program is a fun path to leadership for you and a polite, happy pet. With this program, your puppy will know more by the end of one week than most of your friends' adult dogs learn their entire lives. And you'll have quickly formed the solid foundation for a strong partnership.

5.1.1 What does leadership really mean?

We've all heard that to be a good dog owner you have to be a leader. I don't disagree, but it's important to know that you have a choice about how you want to lead. Some people lead through force and coercion, by being the dictatorial boss. Both animal behavior scientists and schools of marketing and leadership recommend leading more like Mahatma Gandhi, by providing rewards and motivators that followers want to earn. It's a more effective way to lead, as well as being kinder.

With animals, there's an additional component of physical communication (body language), as well. So with dogs, I think of leadership not like being the boss, but more like leading a partner in a dance. In a dance, the lead (usually the man) guides the follow (usually the woman) to perform a sequence of steps. The only way the follow knows what's coming next is that a split second before a move, the lead leads her. He does so not by shouting out words, but by guiding her with subtle body movements. If at any point he daydreams and forgets what he's going to do, the follow immediately knows and may be confused for an instant. If he is consistent in how he signals and his signals are clear, so that she understands, then she will trust his ability to lead her and they will form a stronger relationship. On the other hand, if he frequently forgets to lead or his signals are muddled, then the follow will feel the need to take the lead herself. Then it's just two people dancing near each other but not actually together (See video of leading like a leader in a dance, www.drsophiayin.com).

The same principle applies to training puppies and adult dogs. They have to understand what we want, and the only way that they can is if we provide clear cues and signals. Anyone can do this if we:

- **Set clear house rules** so that we can be consistent about what is expected instead of constantly changing them and confusing our pet. In this program, the rules are that the puppy must say please by automatically sitting for everything she wants.

- **Communicate the rules by rewarding correct behavior** as the puppy does it and removing rewards for unwanted behaviors.

- **Stick to the plan** until the new behavior patterns become habit, rather than just a trick performed for food.

The trick about forming habits in your house is that **while you can train each of the behaviors in this book in just 5 to 10 minutes, to make the behaviors a habit you have be aware that you're training your dog during every single interaction you have with her—whether you know it or not. If you're not aware of what you are doing, you may be training undesirable behaviors more often than desirable ones.** That's why the Learn to Earn program is so important. Our goal is to make good behavior a consistent habit, rather than a trick the puppy performs only when you bring out a treat or a behavior she performs only when you yell or threaten with enough force.

This structured program is what makes the training go so fast. By rewarding polite behaviors all the time and never rewarding the undesirable ones, puppy quickly learns to be polite all the time.

Fig. 5.1.1A

In this program we'll use everything your puppy wants to our advantage as rewards for training purposes. She'll Learn to Earn everything she wants by politely sitting and asking for it. And she'll learn that undesirable behaviors such as jumping on you result in absolutely no rewards—no kibble, no treats, toys, play, talking, petting, going outside, etc.

Fig. 5.1.1B

She'll earn every single kibble. For the fastest training, that means no food in a food bowl. Instead, your pup is going to earn every bit of kibble during training and for learning tricks. Dumping food in a bowl is for people who are too lazy to spend quality time training and interacting with their pet. It's analogous to plopping a kid in front of the TV instead of reading a book to them.

5.1.2 What your puppy will learn.

Besides getting your puppy trained really quickly, this program has many other benefits. By saying please for everything she wants, your puppy will learn:

- **Emotional self control:** That she gets things by being calm and polite, not by whining and working herself into an anxious or overly excited state.

- **Impulse control:** That she should sit politely and ask you, rather than just taking things for herself.

- **That you are fun and worth listening to:** Instead of you yelling and commanding to deaf ears, you'll be able to speak softly because your pup will be tuned in to your voice.

- **To look to you for guidance:** Especially when she doesn't already know what to do.

Best of all, you'll open a clear line of communication and your puppy will be waiting on your every word.

5.1.3 How many weeks does the puppy have to be tethered?

In the beginning, we start puppies on a leash so they don't have a chance to get rewards for unwanted behaviors. Your puppy should remain tethered to you with a hands free leash such as the Buddy System, until she's completely potty trained in the house (that takes a minimum of one month). Once your dog is potty trained, and when she automatically and quickly sits for everything she wants, have her wear her leash but don't attach it to you. Rather, let her drag the leash throughout the house. She should drag a leash around the house until she has a 100% solid come when called, the first time you call, even when there are distractions in the house. Have her wear the leash in the house only when you are home, because it is possible for dogs to get their leashes caught in the furniture and get stuck. Having the dog wear a harness and attaching the leash to the harness instead of the neck collar for this part of the training is a good option.

Once you have the 100% solid come, the puppy doesn't need to wear a leash in the house but she still has to sit for everything she wants. Puppies will stay on leash in the house due to the potty training program much longer than they will need to be leashed for the Learn to Earn program.

The necessity and benefits of tethering: Your puppy should be tethered to you on leash at all times when she isn't in her crate or pen or tethered to an object near you. This works well for potty training, but is also important for teaching her to stick with you and that she can't blow you off. Some pups will wander away when they can't get what they want, and as a result, they reward themselves with something else. Tethering enables you to supervise her directly and to make sure that she only has the opportunity to chew her toys rather than inappropriate objects. I use a hands free leash called the Buddy System (www.Buddysys.com) because it's way more convenient than using a traditional leash.

Fig. 5.1.3A

5.1.4 How long does the whole Learn to Earn program take?

Puppies can get to off-leash privileges as soon as they are potty trained, but should continue to sit for everything they want until it's a habit and until you have the perfect indoor-outdoor pup. When you have a perfectly behaved puppy who sits and asks you for everything she wants, you can give her privileges for free. That is, you'll still want her to sit for all petting, treats, toy tosses and to go out the door for now. But once she's a perfect canine good citizen who greets politely, always comes when called and plays nicely with her toys and not your shoes, you can allow her to jump on you when you invite her to do so with an "up" cue and she can stand and wait at the door instead of having to sit to go out.

When she's perfect, you can even allow her on the furniture if you want, if she asks politely by sitting. Save that privilege until she learns that being on the floor and in her bed and crate are good. Also wait until she's completely potty trained and will immediately get off the furniture when asked. Generally, wait until she's over six months of age to grant this privilege—if you are planning to grant it at all. And remember, if she develops a habit of jumping on furniture without asking, she's not likely to be welcome in other people's homes.

5.2 The Foundation: Say Please by Sitting and Looking at You.

5.2.1 Say please by sitting for treats (kibble).

Good behavior starts by teaching your puppy to automatically say please by sitting. This is the foundation exercise for the Learn to Earn program. By using her entire meal for training, Lucy will get at least 100 rewards for good behavior per day. That means that she'll learn this and other exercises at super-speed.

Fig. 5.2.1A

Fig. 5.2.1B

Fig. 5.2.1C

STEP 1 | Remove your attention when she jumps: Start with a bit of her kibble in your hand. Hold your hand at your belly button. When the puppy jumps on you, stand up straight and be silent so it's clear to her that you're ignoring her (that is, you've removed the reward for jumping, which is your attention) (Figure 5.2.1A). Once she realizes you're not going to reward her for rude jumping behavior she will sit (Figure 5.2.1B)

STEP 2 | When she sits, give her a treat: Be sure your movements are crystal clear. When you hold the treat against your belly button, to her that should signal no treat yet. When she sits, immediately put the kibble in her mouth.

Follow with several more treats while she remains seated, to reward her for continued sitting. Then quickly move several steps away in a way that makes her want to hurry after you, and repeat. Perform these sits repeatedly. When the puppy can do these repeat sits 5 to 10 times in a row, go on to the next exercise.

What can go wrong?

Fig. 5.2.1D
INCORRECT: Avoid bending over your puppy when she's just learning: Bending over her is a cue for her to jump to get to you.

Fig. 5.2.1E
INCORRECT: Avoid holding the treat too high or you'll lure her to jump and even to grab treats roughly.

Fig. 5.2.1F

The right way to deliver treats: To give the treat (kibble), bend your legs while keeping your upper body as straight as possible since leaning may lure her to jump. It should feel as if you're carrying a baby and don't want to bend over. Then just straighten your treat delivery arm so that the treat is delivered right up to her mouth—actually, you should aim to push the treat into her mouth, and hold it there for an instant so you're sure the hand-off is good.

Treat Delivery Tip

- Try to get the treat to your puppy within a second of her good behavior. Dogs and other animals learn best when they get the reward while they're performing the correct behavior. That means you must get the reward to them within a split second and before they start performing another behavior.

- To get the treats to her fast, think of straightening your arm fast, as if you're having an involuntary arm spasm. Or you can think of it as trying to press a game show buzzer when you know the answer and need to ring in faster than your opponent. The speed will make the game more fun for your puppy and she'll want to pay more attention.

- Deliver the treats right to her mouth. Think of even putting a treat right in her mouth and holding it there for second so that you're sure she has it. That way you will avoid accidentally holding the treat too far away and luring her to stand or jump to get it. It will also ensure she doesn't drop the treat. Dropping the treat will train her to look down instead of at you.

5.2.2 Turn sit into a game.

Training isn't about just giving food rewards, it's about making the exercises seem like play. That means we have to add speed, quick changes of directions, and exercises in rapid succession to keep the pup's attention on us. Once dogs figure out that we're really fun, we don't have to work so hard to keep their attention. In general, keep this in mind: Dogs like MTV, not Masterpiece Theater. If they get bored with the training, it's not necessarily because they have a short attention span, it's often because the show (and the human in charge) is boring and there are too many long "commercial breaks." After all, puppies can play with each other for hours on end, because other puppies are fun.

In this section we'll turn sit into a fun game of red light–green light or suddenly settle, by adding speed and then suddenly stopping.

"Dogs like MTV, not Masterpiece Theater. If they get bored with the training, it's not necessarily because they have a short attention span, it's often because the show (and the human in charge) is boring and there are too many long "commercial breaks."

Fig. 5.2.2A

STEP 1 | **Suddenly settle, or follow me and sit:** Start with puppy in a sit.

Fig. 5.2.2B

STEP 2 | **Suddenly settle, or follow me and sit:** Run several steps away, so she chases you. Do not give her any commands; just run so she wants to chase you.

Fig. 5.2.2C

Fig. 5.2.2D

STEP 3 | **Suddenly settle, or follow me and sit:** Stop. Stand still like a tree if the puppy jumps. And then reward her when she sits (Figure 5.2.2C, D). This game is the precursor to a fantastic come when called. Do not work on come when called until she performs this game well.

When your puppy consistently runs after you and then immediately sits when she catches up, you can add her name and a cue to the game if you want. Say her name right before you run, so that "name, come" predicts that something really fun will happen and she should immediately look at you and follow. Only use her name when you know she will respond by looking at and approaching you. If you ever use her name and she ignores you, she's learning that her name is not important. So for now and until her response is a habit, her name must be followed by something fun, such as you running, followed by a treat.

Tip: Dealing with Puppies Who Love to Jump

You can prevent jumping in a dog who really loves to jump by using a "flash lure." That is, when you stop, quickly whip your treat hand down to her nose level before she has caught up, so she stops. When she stops to sniff the treat, raise your treat hand without giving her the treat such that she understands she can't have it yet and then offers a sit. Then give her the treat before she has a chance to jump. Give her several additional treats for remaining seated. So your hand + treat are acting like a stop sign to get her attention and get her to stop, but she does not get to eat the treat until she sits (which she will do if you then hold the treat away from her).

5.2.3 Say please even when humans are crouching.

When humans are in a crouching position, dogs and puppies are more likely to jump on them. Remove all rewards for jumping and reward sit instead.

Fig. 5.2.3A   Fig. 5.2.3B

When you're down at her level, your puppy's more likely to jump on you.

Fig. 5.2.3C

Fig. 5.2.3D

STEP 1 | **Remove your attention or remove the puppy's ability to prop herself on you:** As Lucy starts to jump, I just move my knee (or whatever body part she's planning to jump on) so that she has nothing on which to balance her front legs. Alternatively, I could remove my attention by standing up. The goal is that it's absolutely clear to her that jumping doesn't work and it's clear immediately as she starts to jump, not one or two seconds later. In general avoid pushing her to get her off because when people do this they tend to do it in a way that the puppy interprets as play and attention.

Fig. 5.2.3E

Fig. 5.2.3F

Fig. 5.2.3G

STEP 2 | **Remain stationary until she sits.** Here Lucy sits immediately once she is unsuccessful at propping her front feet on me.

STEP 3 | **Reward the puppy once she sits.** Reward her with one treat for sitting and additional treats for remaining seated.

Fig. 5.2.3H

INCORRECT: Avoid accidentally rewarding or giving your puppy attention for jumping, or you'll confuse her. She'll think you're not a good leader because you can't make up your mind about what you want, and she will have no concept of your personal space. When she's older and automatically greets everyone politely by sitting, you can train her to place her paws on your lap if you want, but it has to be on your verbal or visual command.

Use a flash lure to prevent jumping

Fig. 5.2.3I

STEP 1 | **Prepare as the puppy is running to you:** Assume that every time she approaches you, especially in an excited state, she'll jump. So be mentally prepared for the next step.

Fig. 5.2.3J

STEP 2 | **Present the flash lure:** Before she reaches you and well before she has a chance to jump, suddenly shove your treat hand out into her face like a stop sign to block her from jumping and to get her attention.

Fig. 5.2.3K

STEP 3 | **Reward her for stopping and then for sitting:** Once she's stopped, you can give her that treat and then reward with a second treat for sitting. Or you can just withhold the first treat until she sits. The goal is to practice this so much within several days that she automatically sits without needing the flash lure.

5.2.4 Now reward her for sitting throughout the day.

Practice Tips

- Have random play/training sessions throughout the day where you practice the exercises already shown. Then, throughout the rest of the day, work on the additional Learn to Earn exercises.

- Throughout much of the day, your puppy will be attached by leash to you. As you walk around the house, she'll come with you. Randomly stop and reward her before she starts to pull, and when you're standing around doing dishes or checking your laundry, be prepared to reward her frequently for sitting.

Fig. 5.2.4A
When you walk around the house with your puppy tethered to you, ideally she should sit whenever you stop for a while. So be on the lookout and when she does sit, hurry up and reward her. I can reward her with treats or petting here.

Fig. 5.2.4B
Here Lucy's tethered near me as I work, and I randomly reward her for sitting or lying down quietly. Better to reward her for good behavior so she doesn't have a chance to perform naughty behavior. I'm rewarding her with petting here instead of treats. I can tell she likes it because she's rubbing against me.

5.3 For What Else Should She Say Please?

Once your puppy gets the idea from the previous exercises that sitting is really fun (all of these exercises so far took Lucy only 10 minutes to learn), you can now require her to automatically sit for everything she wants throughout the day.

5.3.1 Say please to be petted.

This is the most difficult exercise for people, because humans always pet dogs without thinking. As a result, people spend more time rewarding naughty jumping behavior (or pre-behaviors) than rewarding quiet sit behavior. If you want a dog who greets everyone by sitting politely instead of jumping, it's important to remove attention when she performs any type of attention-seeking behavior, such as pawing you, barking at you or rubbing against you, as well as actually jumping on you.

Fig. 5.3.1A

Say please to be petted: Here Lucy automatically sits because I don't pet her until she offers the sit. As soon as she sits, I pet her. If your pup starts to jump, remove your petting hand and even get up. Do whatever makes it clear to her that you are removing the reward for petting when she jumps. Avoid pushing her or otherwise interacting with her because attention is a reward. Then, when she sits, reward her with one treat for sitting and additional treats for remaining seated.

Fig. 5.3.1B

Say please to be petted: For pups who nibble on your hands or get excited when you start to pet, start by petting only when you're giving treats. That is, give kibble and pet simultaneously, and then stop doing both at the same time. Then repeat. When she's sitting more calmly, give treats while petting but wait more and more time between each treat.

5.3.2 Say please to go in and out of the house.

Fig. 5.3.2A

Fig. 5.3.2B

Fig. 5.3.2C

Sit to go out the door: Rather than barreling out ahead of you, your pup must remain seated even if the door opens. When I want her to go through, I'll say "okay" or "let's go" and then walk through to guide her through.

Note: If she has to really go potty, better to just run outside so she doesn't have an accident.

Sit to come back into the house: After a short walk outside, I wait by the front door until Lucy sits and looks at me (Figure 5.3.2B). I give her one treat for sitting and a few more for remaining seated (Figure 5.3.2C). Once she has a stable sit and watches me, I open the door and we walk in. By the end of the week, I don't even need to reward with treats. I can reward with petting or praise because Lucy loves both.

Practice Tips

- When giving multiple or sequential treats for sitting make sure you retract your hand and arm and stand up straight between treats rather than keeping your hand near the face the entire time. If you do the latter it will resemble one long treat rather than multiple treats for continued good behavior.

5.3.3 Say please to come in with the people.

When I left Lucy in the yard on her own for the first time, she pawed and jumped and whined at the glass door and I thought, "Uh-oh. She'll develop frustration and anxiety when separated by a barrier or won't be able to be left alone if my parents aren't careful." But with all of the other Learn to Earn exercises for impulse control, by day three she was no longer jumping at the door. Instead, she sat politely to be let back in.

It's essential dogs learn it's okay to be left alone in the yard, in a room or in a carrier or crate. You may have guests or need to separate your pets from other animals or kids. If the pup doesn't learn that it's okay to be alone, she may develop ever-increasing anxiety.

Fig. 5.3.3A

Never reward jumping or barking to be let in. In fact, if the puppy jumps on the door to come in and you're worried about door damage, place an exercise pen or other barrier in front of it so that she doesn't have the opportunity to jump on the door, until you can spend several sessions training her that jumping doesn't work. Otherwise, you'll end up with a 40-pound barking dog who hurls herself against barriers that separate her from being where she wants to be.

Fig. 5.3.3B

Once she sits you can let her in. If she has a jumping habit, practice rewarding her many times with treats for sitting outside and then let her in. For this particular behavior, you'll have to set up the situation so that you can practice many, many times over the course of a few days. If you only practice this several times a day, it may take forever for her to get the message.

5.3.4 Say please to play fetch.

Lucy already likes to run after a toy and bring it back. Fetch is an important game to cultivate in any pup who is active. The short sprints are a more efficient way to exercise your dog than taking her on a walk, even at a brisk pace. For instance, my Jack Russell Terrier can easily run 10 miles with me and look like he hasn't even exercised yet. But after playing fetch he needs to take breaks.

You can turn a game of "toss the toy" into fetch by regularly giving the puppy treats when she brings the toy back, or by putting her on leash and practicing a come when called after she's grabbed the toy.

Fig. 5.3.4A

STEP 1 | **Wait for you puppy to sit before tossing the toy:** Show her the toy but hold it far enough out of her reach that she does not try to jump. If she does try to jump, pull it away further so it's clear that her jumping removed the toy.

Fig. 5.3.4B

STEP 2 | **Toss the toy:** When she sits, to make it clear to her that sitting is what earns the toy, toss it for her.

Fig. 5.3.4C

STEP 3 | **Reward your puppy when she brings it back by playing tug.** The purpose of playing tug is to keep her interested in the toy. Alternatively you can go directly to the next step.

Fig. 5.3.4D

Fig. 5.3.4E

Fig. 5.3.4F

STEP 4 | Stop tugging the toy: To get her to release the toy stop tugging. Often this will get her to relax and let it go, because she's already worked on the say please by sitting exercise and is in a habit of sitting when attention and play stop, she is likely to relax and let go within a couple of seconds after you stop tugging the toy.

STEP 5 | Trade for a high value treat: If step 4 alone doesn't work, then show your puppy a treat and even put it right in her mouth. Make sure the treat is large enough and of high enough value for this situation so that she releases quickly.

STEP 6 | Hold the toy out of range: Once she releases quickly hold the toy out of her range so she doesn't grab it right back. Then you can give her a few additional treats and then repeat the entire game. When she reliably starts releasing the toy immediately with either of these two methods, start saying the word "out" right before you get her to release the toy. "Out" will come to mean "open your mouth and drop the object you're holding."

5.3.5 Say please to get your attention when tethered away from you.

This is great for teaching calm behavior to puppies prone to separation anxiety or dogs who jump, especially to greet you. So if you have a dog who barks for your attention when she's tethered or away from you, or you want to prevent this undesirable habit from developing, do this exercise.

Sit to get attention when tethered.

Fig. 5.3.5A

Fig. 5.3.5B

Fig. 5.3.5C

Tethering a puppy away from you suddenly makes you a valued resource—one the dog no longer can get to at will. With a pup who whines when she can't get to you at will, tether her away from you and wait until she sits (Figure 5.3.5A,B). Then approach and reward her (Figure 5.3.5C). I'm rewarding this dog with petting because he likes being petted. The goal is for the dog to learn that calm, focused behavior is what earns the reward, not whiney, barking, anxious behavior.

5.3.6 Say please to greet people.

I wanted to provide Lucy with many positive experiences with many new people, but at the same time she had to learn to sit to greet them rather than jumping on them. Even puppies can cause harm by jumping. Their sharp nails can scratch, especially people with thin or delicate skin. Since you can't rely on other people to greet your puppy correctly (so she doesn't get rewarded for jumping), you'll have to take control.

Fig. 5.3.6A

Fig. 5.3.6B

Fig. 5.3.6C

STEP 1 | Prepare your puppy for the greeting: When someone wants to greet your puppy, tell the person, "Wait, let me get her to sit first" (Figure 5.3.6A). You may need to make the "halt" signal with your hand to keep the approaching person away. Then get your puppy's attention and have her sit (Figure 5.3.6B). You'll need to get down to her level before you allow the guest to squat down and pet her (Figure 5.3.6C).

Practice Tip: Halt Signal

- You may need to make a halt signal with your hand to keep a potential greeter from approaching until you've prepared your puppy for the greeting by having him sit.

Fig. 5.3.6D

STEP 2 | **Start feeding treats:** Start feeding treats before the greeter reaches out to pet your puppy. Keep your hands at the puppy's face so that she has a steady stream of treats with no time between treats. To do this, you can use two hands so you can hold more treats. Let the person pet her while you feed the treats.

Fig. 5.3.6E

STEP 3 | **Then let the greeter start petting:** Once you're sure your puppy is focused on the treats and not the person, tell the person she can pet her. Keep a steady stream of treats until your puppy is calm.

Fig. 5.3.6F

STEP 4 | **Slow the treat rate down:** Then slow the treat rate down by pulling your treat holding hands far enough away so they are out of reach and the puppy does not try to follow your hands.

Fig. 5.3.6G

STEP 5 | **Reward your puppy before she gets up.** Hurry and give another treat before she starts wiggling or gets up. Gradually increase the interval between treats as long as she remains calm. When the calm greeting becomes a habit you will no longer need treats. Petting is the reward.

Fig. 5.3.6H

Fig. 5.3.6I

INCORRECT: **This is what happens without a steady stream of treats:** If your dog is wiggly and you are not giving a steady stream of treats, as soon as you remove your treat hand from her face to get another treat, she'll turn and jump on the person who's petting her (Figure 5.3.6I)!

Tip: Hands at Dog's Face vs. Away

Fig. 5.3.6J

TIP 1: It helps to hold your dog's collar or leash: To help keep her from jumping, you can hold your dog's collar loosely or hold the leash short while giving treats with the other hand.

TIP 2: **Make sure you're holding treats up to the dog's face** in a position that keeps her in a sit rather than in a position that lures her to reach forward and then get up. Placement of the treat determines where her head will be.

5.4 Three Versions of Leave-it and How to Use Them.

Leave-it is great for teaching your puppy that unwanted, impulsive behaviors don't work. Only saying please by sitting will get her what she wants.

5.4.1 Version 1: Waiting politely to take treats from your hand.

This exercise has three uses.

- In a new situation, your pup learns that pushy, impulsive grabbing doesn't work and she should try something else.

- She learns to take treats nicely instead of grabbing like a land-shark.

- She learns a cue such as leave-it means "take your smelly nose away from my hand and look at me for direction about how to get what you want." Note that this is in contrast to the way many people use leave-it to mean, you never get that. Some dogs that get the "you never get the taboo item" message will want that taboo item even more.

"The message the pup should learn is that if she takes her nose away from the desired object (such as your hand with the treat) and sits and looks at you for direction, she may get the item she wanted. She surely will not get the treat otherwise."

Fig. 5.4.1A

Fig. 5.4.1B

Fig. 5.4.1C

STEP 1 | **Hold your treat hand up to her face:** Start with your dog sitting or lying down so that she won't be moving all over the place. Then hold your treat-filled fist up to her face. She'll most likely sniff and lick and even gnaw at your hand. Just wait it out and hold your hand completely still.

STEP 2 | **Watch for her to move her nose away from your hand:** She will eventually move her nose away from your hand. Some dogs even pause for an instant and look at the hand as if trying to solve the puzzle. Watch carefully for this because it may be quick.

STEP 3 | **Reward her with the treat:** Once she's removed her nose from you hand, open your hand and give her the treat.

Practice Tips

- For this exercise to work so that she doesn't just lose interest all together, make sure she's hungry and you have good treats. Alternatively, if your dog is a chow hound you can start with a lower value treat, as long as when she pulls her head away, she doesn't lose interest and start doing something completely different.

Fig. 5.4.1D

STEP 1 | Leave-it version 1: Start with your food-filled hand near you puppy's mouth: Lucy immediately goes for the treats.

Fig. 5.4.1E

STEP 2 | Leave-it version 1: Watch for her to move her nose away. Because she's still interested in the food, when she pulls her head away in puzzlement, she's still looking at my hand.

Fig. 5.4.1F

STEP 3 | Leave-it version 1: Reward her: I immediately open my hand and let her have the treat.

When you feel pretty comfortable with this exercise, you can start using a release word such as "okay" or "free" or "done" in a unique tone of voice right before you open your hand to give a treat. This release word will mean "go ahead and do what you want; the exercise is done." Most dogs will want to eat the treat in your open hand.

You can also start waiting for your puppy to hold her head away from your hand for longer periods. It's best if you can work up to two to five seconds. Or just go on to the next step of getting good eye contact.

The next step is to work on getting and rewarding eye contact. The goal here is to get your puppy to look away from your hand and up at you and wait patiently for your direction.

Fig. 5.4.1G

Fig. 5.4.1H

Fig. 5.4.1I

STEP 4 | Leave-it version 1: **Place your treat hand near your puppy's face:** Hold one hand with a treat at your forehead and hold the decoy hand (a treat in your fist) in front of the puppy.

STEP 5 | Leave-it version 1: **Wait for her to remove her nose from you hand.** Since she's already had some practice with this exercise, she'll probably remove her nose from your fist pretty quickly.

STEP 6 | Leave-it version 1: **Reward her when she removes her nose from your hand:** When she pulls her nose away from your hand, immediately, say "yes" give the treat from your forehead within a split second. The "yes" will come to indicate to her that she's done something right and a treat is on its way. Because the treat is coming from above, generally after practicing 5 to 20 times in a row your puppy will start looking up in that direction automatically.

Practice Tips

- If you have kids and your puppy likes to grab harshly or gets up as the kids deliver the treat, use the version of leave-it regularly.

- Train everyone to always deliver treats with a closed fist and to only open their fist when they are ready to give the treat. Train the puppy that sitting patiently and looking at them makes the fist magically open so she can have her reward.

When to reward from the hand near her nose.

Fig. 5.4.1J

Fig. 5.4.1K

Fig. 5.4.1L

STEP 7 | **Leave-it version 1: When she consistently looks at your forehead:** When she gets to the point where she consistently looks in the direction of your forehead when you present her with the treat in your fist, you can give the treat from the hand near your head first.

STEP 8 | **Leave-it version 1:** Give the treat from your fist too.

Next train her to look at your face without using a lure near your forehead.

Fig. 5.4.1M

Fig. 5.4.1N

Fig. 5.4.1O

STEP 9 | **Leave-it version 1: Reward her for looking at your eyes:** Now work on rewarding her for looking at your eyes, even without the treat lure near your face. When she removes her nose from your hand and looks up at your face, immediately say "yes" and open your fist hand so she can get the treat.

At this point you can put this behavior on cue using a cue such as "leave-it," or you can expect her to automatically take treats nicely from you and anyone else who hands her a treat in a closed fist. If you have kids or your puppy likes to grab harshly, I recommend that you train her to automatically take the treat nicely from everyone without needing a cue.

5.4.2 Version 2: Blocking her from getting to food on the ground.

This version teaches the dog four things.

- When she can't get what she wants, she should sit and look at you and then maybe you'll give it to her.

- When you block her, she cannot get by so she shouldn't even try.

- When there's food on the ground, she should leave it—either on your cue or automatically, depending on what you decide you want.

- When you give the release word such as "okay," she can do what she wants— which is probably to get the food on the ground.

Fig. 5.4.2A   Fig. 5.4.2B

STEP 1 | **Leave-it version 2: Drop the treat behind you:** It's best to wear a hands-free leash during this exercise instead of holding the leash in your hands so you don't subconsciously do weird things with the leash. With your puppy standing or sitting in front of you, drop the treat to the side and behind you. Make sure the treat is big enough for her to see.

Fig. 5.4.2C

Fig. 5.4.2D

STEP 2 | **Leave-it version 2: Block her from getting to the treat:** When the puppy moves forward to try to get to it, step in front of her as if you're doing a basketball block (Figure 5.4.2C-D). That means you're not allowed to grab the leash. Every time she tries to outmaneuver you and get around you, just step in front of her. If you have a quick puppy, you may want to try this in a hallway or with a wall on one side of you to help limit her movement.

Fig. 5.4.2E

Fig. 5.4.2F

STEP 3 | **Leave-it version 2: Wait for her to sit:** Eventually, if you clearly outmaneuver her (which should be easy if she's really young and uncoordinated), she'll finally figure it out and look to you for guidance—and then sit.

Fig. 5.4.2G

Fig. 5.4.2H

Fig. 5.4.2I

STEP 4 | **Leave-it version 2: Reward her when she sits:** As soon as she sits, give her a treat from your hand. Make sure you do so before she has a chance to get up. Then give her a sequence of treats making sure you stand up straight between each treat. Continue the sequence of treats until she's totally focused on you and no longer tries to look at the treat on the ground.

Fig. 5.4.2J

Fig. 5.4.2K

STEP 5 | **Leave-it version 2: Give her a clear path to the treats:** Then make the task more difficult by standing to the side so she has a clear path to the treat. If she looks at the treat, smooch to her to see if she'll look up.

STEP 6 | **Leave-it version 2: Reward her when she looks up:** If she looks up at you, reward her immediately.

Fig. 5.4.2L

Fig. 5.4.2M

STEP 7 | **Leave-it version 2: Block her if she gets up:** If she starts to get up, block her so it's clear to her that she can't get to the treat .

Fig. 5.4.2N

Fig. 5.4.2O

STEP 8 | **Leave-it version 2: Wait until she sits:** When she's sure she can't get past your block, she'll sit.

Fig. 5.4.2P

Fig. 5.4.2Q

STEP 9 | Leave-it version 2: **Reward sitting before she has a chance to get up** and then follow with a sequence of treats until she's just focused on you.

Fig. 5.4.2R

Fig. 5.4.2S

Fig. 5.4.2T

STEP 10 | Leave-it version 2: **Release her to get the treat:** After her last treat wait two more seconds and, as her final reward for continuing to look at you (Figure 5.4.2S), tell her "okay" or your release word while you point at the food on the ground (Figure 5.4.2T).

Fig. 5.4.2U

Fig. 5.4.2V

Fig. 5.4.2W

STEP 11 | Leave-it version 2: **Let her get to the treat on a loose leash:** Let her get the treat on the ground. Make sure you are close enough to the treat so that she's always on a loose leash and does not get any practice pulling on the leash. Practice this exercise until she consistently sits within a second of your blocking her and remains seated until you say okay. At that point, you can give her fewer treats for the same polite behavior.

> "*Practice this exercise until your puppy consistently sits within a second of your blocking her and remains seated until you say okay.*"

Now you're ready to add the cue "leave-it." Say "leave-it" right after you toss the treat. Only say it once throughout the entire exercise, even if she gets up and you have to block her. She will come to learn "leave-it" means she should get her nose or attention away from the object of interest and sit in front of you for something better. The goal is to form the habit or idea in her mind that there's no need to rush; she's going to get what's on the ground anyway (or a treat from your hand instead).

When your puppy becomes consistent with sitting and looking at you, switch to using a variable rate of reinforcement for dispensing rewards. This means sometimes she gets treats from your hand and sometimes she doesn't. Sometimes she gets the treat on the ground and sometimes she doesn't. Sometimes she gets no treats at all. Because she never knows exactly which time the reward will come, but she knows that it comes sometimes, she'll try harder. She is now on the same type of reward ratio that lures people to keep gambling.

The Variable Reward Schedule (The Power of Gambling)

When animals are first learning a new behavior such as sitting politely everytime you stop on a walk, it's best to reward them immediately and every single time they get the task right and to be sure you never accidentally reward the undesired behavior. By being consistent, you make it clear what you want. Once the puppy knows the behavior well, you can strengthen the behavior even more by going to a variable schedule of reward. In this situation, you reward, on average every second, third, fourth or more, times she does the behavior correctly but not exactly every second, third, or fourth time. Sometimes she may get rewarded each time she performs the behavior and sometimes she gets rewarded the fifth time she performs the behavior correctly. That way she never knows exactly which time she's going to get rewarded for her desired behavior that she already knows pretty well. This predictably unpredictable schedule of rewards has been shown to be the strongest schedule of reinforcement. In fact it's one reason people enjoy gambling. They may see that the odds of winning are good, but they don't know exactly which time they will win.

Practice Tips

- If you decide that your puppy should never be allowed to pick taboo items up off the ground, then instead of releasing her to pick up the treat on the ground, pick it up yourself and hand it to her. When might this version be useful? You may use it if you have a puppy who spends excessive time picking up taboo items off the ground during walks and eating them, or if you have two pets who might fight over dropped food.

- Once your puppy focuses on you well as soon as you start to block, decrease the number of treats you give until you get to the point where you reward primarily with access to the treat on the ground.

- Once she consistently performs the leave-it immediately, you can also move to a variable schedule of reinforcement where you sometimes reward her and other times you do not.

5.4.3 Version 3: Tossing food beyond the range of the leash.

This version of the Learn to Earn exercises also teaches the pup four things. The pup learns:

- When she can't get what she wants, she should sit and look at you and then maybe you'll give it to her.

- When she gets to the end of the leash, she's going nowhere so she should come back and look to you for guidance.

- When there's food on the ground, she should leave it—either on your cue or automatically, depending on what you decide you want.

- When you give the release word such as "okay," she can do what she wants— which is probably to get the food on the ground.

Fig. 5.4.3A

Fig. 5.4.3B

STEP 1 | Leave-it version 3: Toss the treat and wait it out: Start with your dog standing or sitting in front of you and toss a treat out of her leash range. Stand completely still so that when she gets to the end of the leash, she won't pull you and learn that pulling works. It's important that she gets a chance to figure out that pulling doesn't work.

Fig. 5.4.3C

Fig. 5.4.3D

Fig. 5.4.3E

Fig. 5.4.3F

Fig. 5.4.3G

STEP 2 | Leave-it version 3: Give sequential rewards when she sits and looks at you: Your dog will eventually turn and sit and look at you, because she's been rewarded for this a lot in the past (Figure 5.4.3 C and D). Reward her immediately when she does (Figure 5.4.3E). Then give her a sequence of treats so that she remains seated and looking at you (5.4.3F and G). Make sure you stand up straight between each treat.

> "*It's important that your puppy gets a chance to learn that pulling doesn't work.*"

Fig. 5.4.3H

Fig. 5.4.3I

STEP 3 | **Leave-it version 3: Release your puppy to get the treat:** When she's just focused on you and not on the ground and holds that focus for 2 seconds, you can tell her "okay" and point to the treat on the ground so she knows she can get it. Or you can pick it up and give it to her if you never want her to pick up things off the ground.

Fig. 5.4.3J

Fig. 5.4.3K

Fig. 5.4.3L

STEP 4 | **Leave-it version 3: Walk over quickly enough so she's on a loose leash:** As soon as you say "okay," move closer to the treat so she does not have the opportunity to pull you.

Fig. 5.4.3M

INCORRECT: Don't let her pull you, or you're teaching her that pulling works. That basically negates what you were just trying to teach her.

What if she gets up and goes back to the treat on her own?

Fig. 5.4.3N

Fig. 5.4.3O

Your puppy may get up prematurely and head back to the treat: If you deliver the treats slowly or too late or don't get sequential treats to your puppy, she may try to go back to the treat on the ground before you have released her. Be consistent. Remain stationary so you do not let her pull you closer to the treat on the ground.

Fig. 5.4.3P

Fig. 5.4.3Q

Fig. 5.4.3R

Fig. 5.4.3S

Wait her out: Again, she'll learn that pulling doesn't work. You can give her a hint if she looks like she's trying to figure it out. Smooch or cluck to her, but just once. When she finally sits give her a series of treats for remaining seated. In general, avoid saying her name unless you are 100% sure she'll look at you. Otherwise you may just teach her to ignore her name.

When she's consistently sitting within one second of you tossing the treat on the ground, you can start using the cue "leave-it" before you toss the treat.

Practice Tip

- Just as we want our kids to learn to say "please" and "thank you" automatically, we want puppies and adult dogs to sit automatically for everything they want. That's why we don't just tell them to sit every time we want it even after they know the cue word "sit." Instead, we make it clear by our action of waiting and rewarding the appropriate behavior that only sitting (their way of saying "please") and looking at you works to get them what they want.

5.4.4 Applying leave-it to toys.

We can apply the same leave-it exercise to self control around toys. This exercise is for dogs who love toys, tug or fetch. Practicing self control around toys means your puppy will not feel the need to go after other dogs' toys, or to run after anything that's tossed anywhere near her.

Fig. 5.4.4A

Fig. 5.4.4B

With your dog sitting (Figure 5.4.4A), toss the toy beyond the range of the leash just the way you did with the treat (Figure 5.4.4B). By now she should know she won't be allowed to run to the end of the leash and pull you to the toy. So at this point there's no need to give a verbal leave-it cue; however, you can give her the leave-it cue just once if you are sure she knows it well—and then stand still in case she does leap for the toy. If she remains seated and looking at you, give her a series of treats, just as when you were doing this exercise by tossing food on the ground.

Fig. 5.4.4C

Fig. 5.4.4D

When she keeps her eyes on you (Figure 5.4.4C), give her the release word and let her get the toy. Be sure to get there fast enough so she's on a loose leash (Figure 5.4.4D).

Fig. 5.4.4E

When she has the toy you can play tug with her, so that she continues to be motivated by toys.

Practice Tip

- It's important for puppies and dogs that go crazy over toys to learn to perform leave-it for their toys and to also learn to sit to have their toy tossed (section 5.3.4). Some people believe that you can train a dog to be well-behaved by exercising him until he's tired. For dogs that go bonkers over their toy, if they are allowed to bark and pace and jump and then their toy is tossed, you are actually rewarding them for this unruly behavior. So regardless of how much exercise they are getting, they are practicing impatience and this will negatively affect their behavior in other high excitement situations.

5.4.5 Using leave-it to wait politely at the door.

You can use one of the leave-it exercises to stop your dog from charging out the door whenever you open it, and to get him to sit to go out on walks. Open the door and be ready to block your dog, just as you did in the leave-it exercise where you tossed food onto the ground behind you.

Fig. 5.4.5A

If your dog tries to go out on his own, quickly block him. Because I want him to learn to sit automatically in this situation, I am not giving him the leave-it command. My body language should say it all, and if he ignores my body language, he would have ignored my verbal leave-it cue, too.

Fig. 5.4.5B

Now I'm standing in front of him. This is like a basketball block. I do not grab his leash; instead, I physically show him that I can outmaneuver him with my body by just stepping in front of him.

Fig. 5.4.5C
He finally sits. Sit is his default behavior, because he's been rewarded so many times with treats for sitting.

Fig. 5.4.5D
Now I reward him with petting before I give him the release word and let him walk through the door. He must look at me for one to two seconds before I reward him by letting him go out the door.

5.4.6 Practicing in other real-life situations in the home.

For the leave-it exercises to be useful in real life, you have to practice in real-life situations such as when you're preparing food in the kitchen or walking around the house or even when you're on a walk.

Fig. 5.4.6A

Fig. 5.4.6B

Fig. 5.4.6C

During your normal daily activities in the house or on walks drop food as if by accident.

Be ready to block your dog and then reward her only once she sits or lies down and looks at you. If my goal is to have the dog automatically leave any item dropped on the ground, I will not use the cue leave-it. I'll just block her. If I want her to leave the item only on my verbal "leave-it" cue, then once I'm pretty certain she will respond to my block by sitting quickly, I will use the word "leave-it" an instant before I block her. "Leave-it" will be her cue to sit and look at me.

Fig. 5.4.6D

Fig. 5.4.6E

Fig. 5.4.6F

This type of training is very important in locations such as the kitchen, because you may drop something that dogs are not allowed to have such as this grape which may be toxic. Or you may have two dogs who are possessive over dropped food. If you teach them both to never pick up food off the ground and that you'll pick it up for them, you will eliminate that source of conflict.

Note that because you will have put this behavior on a variable ratio of reinforcement, meaning sometimes the dog gets the "taboo" item you're practicing with and sometime she does not, she won't mind not getting the real taboo item because maybe she'll get it next time. As a result, she'll still retain her polite leave-it habit (Figure 5.4.6F).

5.5 When to Add the Cue Word "Sit."

With all of this sitting you probably wonder when to add the cue word to sit. So far we haven't used many words as cues because we want the puppy to learn to say please by sitting automatically rather than being micromanaged. Plus we've been trying to develop good human habits of relying on body language and properly timed rewards to get desired behaviors. Without going through this specific "no-cue" phase, we humans tend to spew words out repeatedly so that they become meaningless to the pet.

Now that you are starting to gain good habits of communicating with your pet, you can teach the cue word "sit" since you may want your puppy to sit in situations where she does not want something from you and that are not part of the learn to earn program.

To teach it, just say "sit" an instant before your puppy's about to sit. For instance if you run with your puppy and then suddenly stop, your puppy should know to sit right as she catches up to you. Say "sit" and instant before she starts to sit. Do this consistently for a couple of days and she'll pick up that the word is related to the action of sitting.

5.6 Turning the Sit Game and Leave-It Into Walking on Leash.

The purpose of the leash is to help your puppy know what her boundaries are. When she is on leash, never let her pull or you will be rewarding her pulling behavior. Also avoid dragging her around. Your goal is to teach her to stay next to you on a loose leash.

5.6.1 Walking on leash in the heel position.

When you first put a pup on leash, she may just stand still and not want to walk. Similarly, even after the puppy walks on leash in the house, when she first goes outside into unfamiliar territory, she is more likely to hang back. That makes training her to heel (walk on your left side with her front feet even with or slightly behind you) easy in pups, at least for the first couple of days. In fact, it's ideal to train her to heel before she has a chance to learn to pull. Lucy's already good on leash in the house because she's been tethered to me in the house for several days and has been rewarded a lot for following me and then sitting. On her first walk outside; however, she was scared, which provided an opportunity for me to show you how to train a puppy who's nervous to follow on leash.

Fig. 5.6.1A

Fig. 5.6.1B

Walking on leash: Start with her on your left side (or the right side if you've designated the right as the side on which you want her to regularly walk). Walk a few feet away (Figure 5.6.1A). Because she's learned to follow you and sit so much at home (Refer to section 5.2.2), she should automatically follow you. In fact, it only took Lucy a few minutes on day two to teach her how to follow on leash. If she doesn't follow you, show her the treat by holding it down at her nose level on your left side (Figure 5.6.1B). She'll walk right to you.

Fig. 5.6.1C

When she catches up, you can reward her when she's standing if she's too nervous to sit right away. You probably only need a food lure the first few times; then she should start to feel more confident and follow more readily. Once she's coming more readily, when she catches up wait for her to sit on your left side and then reward her. Then you can switch to rewarding her for walking next to you rather than only rewarding when you've stopped and she sits. You can also sometimes run and suddenly stop, just as you did with the suddenly settle game (Refer to section 5.2.2). This makes walking outside while paying attention to you more fun—like MTV for dogs.

Fig. 5.6.1D

Use other motivators too: When she's nervous, Lucy stops taking treats, so I bring a toy for her to play with in case she gets scared. Lucy has only been on three short walks in my suburban neighborhood and several ventures in other locations, and has not yet experienced buses, loud trucks, streetcars and other loud man-made vehicles. I let her look at the thing that's scaring her, and try to get her into play mode with a toy or by petting her excitedly as if you're playing. Usually, Lucy suddenly gets happy and then will take treats.

5.6.2 Prevent pulling.

The first step in preventing pulling is to make sure your puppy knows just how much leeway she has on the leash. If we're using a conventional leash—you hold it in your hand, rather than a hands-free leash—you have to be careful to choose one leash length and stick with it, rather than accidentally increasing the length by moving your arm. To do this, be sure to keep your leash-holding arm strong against your hip.

Correct: Keep the leash the same length by keeping your wrist glued to your hip.

INCORRECT: Avoid varying the leash length by moving your arm.

Practice Tip

- Some puppies love to grab their leash, especially since it dangles in their face. They pull and want you to play with them by pulling back. This is where the learn to earn really comes into play. If they know learn to earn exercises well then if you stand stationary it will be clear that grabbing the leash doesn't work; you won't play tug with them. Then they will sit and you can reward them with a treat. To keep their mind off grabbing the leash, remind them of the learn to earn games

Where does walking on leash fall within the Learn to Earn program?

- In this Learn to Earn program puppies learn to sit for everything they want—treats/kibble, toys, petting, going out the door. To learn that they will not get rewards for unwanted behaviors such as blowing you off when they can't immediately get what they want, they need to spend time tethered to human family members on leash.

- During Lucy's first week she spent 1-2 hours of our 16 hour day attached to me via hands-free leash while I walked around the house doing chores and various tasks. I made a point to stop frequently so that she could get a lot of practice sitting for treats rather than having a chance to get ahead and pull.

- During other times of the day she was either tethered to furniture near me, in her crate, or playing with me outside. To see an example of our schedule see section 5.9.

Even in the house, your puppy should be walking next to you rather than getting ahead, weaving back and forth, and causing you to trip and fall. So as soon as his front feet get ahead of your feet, just stop so that you are stationary by the time he gets to the end of the leash.

Fig. 5.6.2A   Fig. 5.6.2B

INCORRECT: Never let the dog pull on leash. Remember, every time you're near him, you're training him to do either the right thing or the wrong thing.

Fig. 5.6.2C

Here, when he pulls, I stop before the dog gets to the end of the leash. He thinks, "Hey, nothing's happening, I don't get to go where I want."

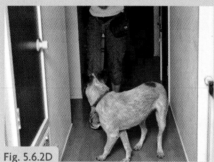

Fig. 5.6.2D

So he comes back. . .

Fig. 5.6.2E

. . . and sits in front of me. Then I can reward him with a treat and walk forward.

5.7 Come When Called.

Because puppies like to follow, they can start off with a virtually 100% perfect recall. Unfortunately, most people mess this up because they spend a lot of time calling their pup—"Rover, Rover, Rover"—when their pup could care less. The puppy just learns to ignore her name and the command to come. Or they think their pup likes to follow them already, so they don't reward the pup's following behavior. Then, when the pup becomes more independent, she no longer cares to follow.

To turn your pup's following response (the one you trained on day one by training her to say please by sitting) into a recall, call the pup only when you know she will come. For instance, if you call her and run the other way, she'll naturally want to chase you. When she does come, make it worth her while. Give her treats, pet her, play with her. You may need to do this with her on leash so that she has no option but to come. If she never has the opportunity to do anything but come running to you when called, and coming is always fun (that is, you don't yell at her and expect her to come running or call her to come so you can end a game), then coming when called, even with a lot of distractions, will become a habit.

"*Because puppies like to follow, they can start off with a virtually 100% perfect recall. Just make sure that coming when called is always fun, it ends with a reward that they like.*

Also make sure that at first you practice with a leash so that the puppy never has the opportunity to do anything but immediately run to you as soon as he hears you call."

5.7.1 Come is an extension of the fun sit exercises.

Fig. 5.7.1A

Fig. 5.7.1B

Come when called: This exercise is just an extension of say please by sitting (Refer to section 5.2.2). First make sure your pup consistently follows you when you run and then sits when she catches up without your needing to guide her with the leash. If you're not sure about this exercise, go back and practice some more. When you're 100% sure she'll follow you in this game, say "Lucy come" (substitute your dog's name, of course!). Say it just once, but in an energetic, encouraging voice, and run a short distance away from her (Figure 5.7.1A). When she catches up to you, reward her after she sits (Figure 5.7.1B).

Practice Tips

- If you're not sure whether your puppy will follow, start with her on leash so that you can coax her a little and at least prevent her from running off.

- If needed, reward her right when she gets to you rather then waiting for her to sit. Then give her more rewards when she sits. If she doesn't follow you 100% of the time, go back to section 5.2.2 and practice some more.

- You can also reward her with praise, petting, or play, whichever she likes at the time you are training.

5.7.2 Come when called, with distractions.

The goal of the previous exercise was to make coming when called fun. When it is, even with distractions your dog will think running when she's called is as fun as what she's already doing. But sometimes to be sure, we need to have the puppy on leash so that she has no other option but to come when called.

Fig. 5.7.2A
Here Lucy wants to explore what Jonesy is eating and Jonesy wants his personal space. I shouldn't leave it up to Jonesy to have to teach Lucy what's right all the time, as that can make Jonesy feel harassed.

Fig. 5.7.2B
I grab onto the leash that Lucy was dragging so I have control. Note that this takes place during a specific session in which I'm watching her closely and letting her wander around the room—because I still have to be careful about her potty training.

Fig. 5.7.2C
Then I call her and head the other direction. I pull gently on her leash to get her facing my way and then show her the treat so she knows where to run.

Fig. 5.7.2D
Since this is a high distraction situation, I'll give her the treat when she's still standing.

Coming when called should be as much fun as playing with another dog or exploring new things. My ultimate goal is to make coming when called so much fun that Lucy immediately runs in my direction full speed the first time she hears me call her. Then I can reward her with treats, petting, praise or whatever she responds to, and then provide an added reward of letting her go back and play.

Fig. 5.7.2E **Here's another example with a cat:** Lucy just met this cat and wants to wrestle and play. The cat doesn't like pushy play behavior and tries to escape.

Fig. 5.7.2F **I hold the leash,** call Lucy and then immediately run in the other direction.

Fig. 5.7.2G

Lucy immediately comes running. When she consistently comes running immediately when called without feeling even a gentle pull on her leash, we can start practicing come when called off leash. Notice that I hold the treats down at her level when she's just learning to perform in this distracting situation.

Also practice having her come away from playmates. When doing so, you can reward her with treats and repeat sits, then let her play with the other dogs again (as long as they're willing!).

5.8 What to Do When Puppy Nips and Chews Inappropriate Objects.

5.8.1 Method 1: Distracting and replacing with an appropriate toy

Puppies love to chew on objects including our shoes, pants, and arms. To them all objects are toys. We can train them to only chew on appropriate toys by providing appropriate toys and redirection play towards them.

Fig. 5.8.1A

Fig. 5.8.1B

Puppies like to chew on clothes and shoes. Here Lucy's chewing my shoelace and my shoe.

Fig. 5.8.1C

Replace the inappropriate object with a more appropriate one: I wave a more appropriate toy in front of her and she grabs it.

Practice Tips

- Make toys more fun by tugging them a little but be able to get your puppy to release it within one second with a food trade so she doesn't learn to get overly aroused.

- Put treats in the toy or toss it around in order to make it more interesting and fun.

- Prevent your puppy from chewing your shoes in the first place by putting a toy in her face as soon as she shows interest in your shoes.

5.8.2 Method 2: Distracting with a treat, rewarding calm sit.

Never let a puppy chew on your arm. If she does, you can try saying "ow!" or "out!" really loud—loud enough to startle her. When she lets go and looks at you, reward her with a treat and then put something more appropriate in her mouth. If "out" works to get her to immediately let go, then it can become her cue word to let go.

Fig. 5.8.2A

Puppies like to grab our waving arms the same way they grab their playmates: Never let a puppy chew on your arm. If she does, you can try saying "ow!" or "out!" really loud—loud enough to startle her. When she lets go and looks at you, reward her with a treat and then put something more appropriate in her mouth. If "out" works to get her to immediately let go, then it can become her cue word to let go.

Fig. 5.8.2B

Lucy doesn't respond to a sharp, loud "ow." The sound does not startle her and make her stop and look at me. So I don't use it with her because it's just wasted breath and clouds the meaning of other words I might use. Instead, I just show her the treat. Since she's used to the food reward routine and is earning all her food by sitting, this works well.

Fig. 5.8.2C

Fig. 5.8.2D

She lets go and I give her the treat (kibble). If she didn't let go, I'd shove the treat in her face so she would be sure to see it. Also make sure the treat is big enough. Next, I put a toy in her mouth and she falls on her back and plays with it.

I can still teach Lucy the cue "out" if I say "out" and immediately push a food treat in her face, so she lets go within one to two seconds of the cue. If I pair the word with a consistent response by her, then the word will take on the meaning "let go." If I say the cue and cannot get a consistent response, then the word will just be babbling noise.

5.9 What a Typical Day on Learn to Earn and Potty Training Program Looks Like.

You know all the exercises now and that the puppy should spend a lot of time attached to family members on leash. Here's an example of how to make polite behavior a habit throughout the day. This is what the first couple of days in the house were like with Lucy.

7 a.m. wake up (15 minutes)	**Potty then play session 1:** Open up Lucy's crate and rush outside before she has a chance to stop and potty in the hallway. She immediately pees when outside, but I stand around not playing with her for 10 minutes until she poops too.
7:15-7:45 a.m. (30 minutes)	**Playtime:** During this time she works for her kibble playing the "chase after me and suddenly sit for a treat" game. Then we work on toy tugging, sit to have toy tossed, and food trades to get the to back. I also pick her up and practice handling her while giving her treats so she learns to enjoy it. She potties again. Then I take her inside. She also has access to water outside.
8-10 a.m.	**Rest in her crate:** where she can't have a potty accident. She has toys to keep her occupied and is playing with them. Note that for short periods I can let her play outside on her own unsupervised if I have a puppy safe and potty appropriate yard.
10-10:15 a.m. (15 minutes)	**Potty then play session 2:** Take her out to potty. This time she goes right away, so I play with her for 10 minutes. Same as the first play session. I let her explore the yard, too.
10:15-noon	**She follows me around the house, attached to me with a hands-free leash:** Whenever I stop and am standing around, if she sits I give her sequential rewards. She's already starting to sit a lot. She lies in her bed by my desk when I work at my computer.
Noon	**Potty then play session 3:** I take her outside. She does not go potty, so I put her in her crate (for 15 minutes) and then take her out again. This time she potties, so she gets some off-leash yard play time again with me for 10 minutes.
12:30-2:30 p.m.	**Attached to me while I work in my office:** She is tethered nearby with toys.

2:30-2:45 p.m. (15 minutes)	**Potty then play session 4:** By now I am rewarding her for her sit behavior with petting instead of treats. Sometimes I reward with petting and other times with treats.
2:45-4 p.m.	**Attached to me:** while I work in my office. Again, she is tethered nearby with toys.
4-5:30 p.m. (1½ hours)	**Potty then play session 5:** She's getting good at sitting to be petted. Now Jonesy gets to run with her outside and get rewarded too. A friend comes over and Lucy gets to practice greeting a new person, plus the friend's dog. They play for more than half an hour.
5:30-7:30 p.m.	**Rest in her crate:** with toys while I have my dinner.
7:30-9:30 p.m.	**Potty then tethered to me:** in the house. I reward her sits with petting or some treats.
9:30-11:30 p.m.	**Potty and play or handling session:** She may sit on my lap in different positions.
11:30 p.m.	**Last potty break:** Then to bed in her crate for the night.

Synopsis of Events in Our 16-hour Day

Number of potty breaks	8
Crate time	**4 hours** (Two 2 hour sessions)
Play and training games outside:	**2.5 hours**
Time spent tethered to me or to furniture near me in the house (such as when I'm working or relaxing).	**8.5 hours**
Time spent tethered to me walking around the house.	**1-2 hours** (of the 8.5 hours)

5.10 A Recap of the Learn to Earn Program.

Just in case your head is spinning here's a quick recap of what the Learn to Earn Program looks like.

5.10.1 Tether your puppy to you during a busy time of day.

Fig. 5.10.1A   Fig. 5.10.1B   Fig. 5.10.1C

Your puppy should be tethered to you via a hands-free leash for at least 1-2 hours a day during a time when you are walking around the house a lot such as when you are tidying, cooking, or cleaning up. It's important that you're walking around the house a lot so that the puppy has a lot of practice learning to learn to walk by your side as you go from place to place and sitting when you stop or stand still.

Fig. 5.10.1D   Fig. 5.10.1E

Sit at doors: Remember that she should also sit to go outside or come back inside.

Sit for petting: She should also sit for all petting and attention.

5.10.2 Tether your puppy to you when you are working at your desk or relaxing.

Fig. 5.10.2A Fig. 5.10.2B

You puppy should also spend time tethered to or near you when you are working or relaxing. You can reward with petting or treats/kibble. Reward frequently enough so she remains sitting or lying down or provide toys for her to play with so she doesn't try to jump on or climb on you or get into other trouble.

5.10.3 Provide play time and work on training games.

She should have plenty of playtime outside in a potty safe area (or inside but when you can watch her for signs that she has to potty).

Fig. 5.10.3A Fig. 5.10.3B

Remember that she must practice desired behaviors even during play. You can have her run after you but when she catches up she should sit.

Fig. 5.10.3C
Fetch: She can also play fetch but must sit before you toss the toy.

Fig. 5.10.3D

Fig. 5.10.3E
Other dogs: She can also play

5.10.4 Where should your puppy be when you need a break from her?

Fig. 5.10.4A

In her crate: Include toys or a food-filled Kong® to keep her entertained. If you use food, be sure it's a portion of her regular daily alotment.

Fig. 5.10.4B

Tethered in the same room but away from you: Make sure she has enough toys to keep her occupied. She does not need to remain seated or lying down in this situation.

In an exercise pen: Only put her here if she's already potty trained or if you have to be gone for long periods of time. In the latter case make one side comfy and set up the other side as a potty area.

Fig. 5.10.4C

Fig. 5.10.4D

In a puppy and potty-safe area outside: She can be placed outside alone for short periods. If she's supervised she can be outside for longer periods.

Fig. 5.10.4E

Sit to come in: When she wants to come in, make sure she asks by sitting quietly.

Practice Tip

- Every time you interact with your puppy you're training her even if you're not aware of it. If you want your puppy to develop good behavior, you'll have to pay attention to your every movement and action around her.

- Each exercise of the Learn to Earn Program takes just minutes to train. To make these new polite behaviors a habit though, you'll need to consistently reward only the desired behaviors and avoid rewarding the unwanted behaviors until they are routine.

Chapter 6

Socializing Your Pup to Dogs, People, New Environments, and Handling

Why is early socialization so essential? »

Why is early socialization so essential? As pointed out in chapter one, three weeks to three months is the sensitive period for socialization in dogs. That means this is the time when the puppy is curious and primed to form social bonds. It's the golden window for Lucy to learn that all kinds of people and dogs, objects, and environments are safe. After this period, her default setting will be to fear everything new. That's why it's important for puppies and their humans to participate in puppy socialization classes.

The more positive experiences your puppy has during this period, the less fearful she will be when facing new things in the future. So during this time, and continuing through at least one year of age, it's important to give her many positive experiences so she can learn that new things are interesting and fun. The reason to continue for so long is that some dogs just need constant practice and others go through a prominent fear period some time between six months and over a year where they are more sensitive to becoming fearful again.

While socialization is essential, it's important, to recognize when your puppy is afraid or has had enough of something new. So at the end of this chapter I'll give you a kind of canine body language visual dictionary to help you recognize fear and anxiety. I'll also give you some advice about how to deal with it.

6.1 Training Puppies to Love Being Handled.

Most of us want to occasionally cuddle and hug our dogs; but what many owners don't know is that while many dogs may tolerate hugging, most do not enjoy it. If you start with handling exercises when your puppy is young, she can learn to not only enjoy the handling needed for everyday healthcare but can learn to enjoy being cuddled and hugged too.

6.1.1 Teach them to enjoy being held in different positions.

Be sure to get them used to every position that you might potentially hold them in. This includes tight cuddling and hugging.

Fig. 6.1.1A   Fig. 6.1.1B   Fig. 6.1.1C   Fig. 6.1.1D

Practice holding her in different positions. Give treats periodically to reward her and to distract her from struggling. If she's likely to struggle give treats faster to distract her and keep her calm. Make sure you hold the treats right up to her face so it encourages her to remain still, rather than holding the treats in a way that causes her to reach for them. Once she's relaxed, slow the treat rate down.

Fig. 6.1.1E

Avoid letting her go when she struggles. Instead, support her well and release her when she relaxes.

Fig. 6.1.1F

Give treats frequently at first if your puppy is uncomfortable with being in a new position.

Fig. 6.1.1G   Fig. 6.1.1H   Fig. 6.1.1I

Lucy struggles at first in this position but she quickly calms down when she realizes she gets treats. It's important to support the puppy well and hold her firmly even when you're giving her treats. She's supported in the groove between the handler's legs and the handler is holding both legs above the elbow.

Fig. 6.1.1J
Within a couple of days Lucy can be picked up and placed in almost any position and she remains relaxed.

You can also use these exercises to help her be an excellent client at the veterinarian's office. Be sure to train her to enjoy getting injections, foot handling, mouth handling, ear handling, toenail trims and being placed in many different positions. Lucy is already good for all of these things, but needs continued practice. (For handling exercises in detail, refer to chapters 18 and 19 of Low Stress Handling, Restraint and Behavior Modification of Dogs & Cats. Visit www.lowstresshandling.com)

6.1.2 Handle your puppy's feet, ears and mouth, as if you're examining them.

Make sure you include all types of handling and care your puppy may need. That includes grooming, cleaning the eyes, the feel of the clippers, brushing their teeth, grabbing their tail, feeling their rear the same way a veterinary technician might prior to inserting a thermometer. At first always pair with food so they have a good experience.

Fig. 6.1.2A
Foot handling: Lucy is receiving a treat as her foot is being squeezed. It's important only at the level where she remains focused on treats. After several successes, we then squeeze more firmly, but still stay below her threshold for reacting.

Fig. 6.1.2B
Toenail Trim: Later we will clip her nails as she's getting a treat as we are with this puppy. Then we will graduate to clipping a nail or 2 followed by giving a treat and work up to clipping all of her nails and rewarding her calm behavior with treats or praise.

Fig. 6.1.2C

Fig. 6.1.2D

Head collar: This is also a great time to train your pup to love wearing a head halter such as the Gentle Leader® Headcollar. The head halter can come in handy early in training because it helps you guide the pup's head and thus her focus back to you. It can be very useful on walks when used correctly. We didn't work on this with Lucy but here's an example with other puppies. Just give the puppy treats through the nose loop until he willingly puts his nose through.

Fig. 6.1.2E

Fig. 6.1.2F

Fig. 6.1.2G

Once you have the head collar on, continue to give treats and distract them so they get used to wearing it. For more details on how to train this download the handout on training dogs to love wearing muzzles at http://drsophiayin.com/professional-resources. The approach is nearly identical.

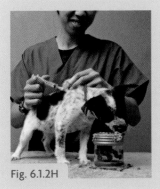

Fig. 6.1.2H

This puppy is getting treats as the technician pokes. As soon as the technician stops poking, she removes the remaining treats. Then she repeats the procedure a bunch of times so that the puppy can learn that treats are specifically associated with being poked and treats stop when the poking stops. As usual the goal is to always stay below the level that causes the puppy to react negatively. The puppy should just be focused on the food.

Practice Tips

• Continue these exercises with each family member and anyone who might care for the puppy even if the puppy has already gone through the exercises with the breeder or others.

• Hold the puppy so she feels secure and can't get loose. Use food to distract her and provide a positive association.

Fig. 6.1.21

Puppies can get better or worse within days: This particular puppy was calm for handling at eight weeks of age. Her new owner; however, would release her whenever she started struggling. Within two days she had learned to growl whenever she didn't want to be handled. After a week of proper handling as described in the chapter by the new owner, the puppy again remained relaxed when held and handled.

6.1.3 Train them that having their collar grabbed is fun.

Gotcha is a collar grab that's important because you never know when you might have to suddenly grab your puppy to get her out of trouble. Many dogs react to sudden grabbing by becoming scared or think they need to defend themselves. By teaching a collar grab, our goal is that the puppy learns that having the collar grabbed is fun.

Fig. 6.1.3A

Fig. 6.1.3B

Fig. 6.1.3C

Practice gotcha so that you can pull her away from distractions: Grab her collar (Figure 6.1.3A) and gently guide her into a big treat (Figures 6.1.3B,C). That way, she learns to associate a collar grab with getting a treat and will enjoy being grabbed in the future, rather than reacting aggressively. Make sure that when you first start this exercise, the treat is fairly close to her head so she doesn't have to be pulled far to get something good. Also make sure the treat is high value to her. When you're sure she's having positive experiences, then hold the treat further away. You know she likes having her collar grabbed when her normal response to your grabbing it is that she turns and looks for a treat or heads to where she thinks you are holding or hiding the treat (in your hand).

6.2 Providing Positive Experiences with Unfamiliar People.

6.2.1 Lucy meets 100 people in 100 days.

To help prevent Lucy from experiencing fear and anxiety when meeting new people, I set a goal to give her positive experiences with 100 different people in 100 days. it's important that the experiences are positive, not just neutral or unknown. So far, in the week I've had her she's met 10 people and liked them all. I avoid having her meet too many people at once since I don't want to overwhelm her.

Fig. 6.2.1A   Fig. 6.2.1B

Have different types of people handle your puppy and give her treats for sitting. Don't risk giving your puppy a neutral or negative experience. To make sure her experience is always positive, make sure she looks happy and relaxed (there's a canine body language guide at the end of this chapter), wants to greet them, and even gets treats or experiences something else positive (such as a toy toss or petting, if she likes that). In these photos Lucy is getting used to people with masks, hats and umbrellas (Figure 6.2.1A), as well as a big biker-mechanic dude (Figure 6.2.1B).

Fig. 6.2.1C
Here Lucy greets a child, Liliana. Liliana's mother gives Lucy treats for sitting so that Lucy doesn't jump.

Fig. 6.2.1D

Fig. 6.2.1E
Lucy sits for Liliana, who already knows how to feed treats to dogs. Even after receiving a treat, Lucy continues to sit patiently while watching Liliana.

Most likely you'll need to give treats continuously to a puppy to keep her from jumping on kids and guests, since these people will not know how to avoid reinforcing jumping behavior (see section 5.3). When your puppy is sitting reliably, you can decrease the rate of treats. Because Lucy's been rewarded so much for sitting, she readily sits and remains seated for Liliana (Figures 6.2.1D, E). And even when she's standing and Liliana starts to pet her, Lucy sits instead of jumping. Of course, if she had just been playing with another dog or was in a new environment, she might not be as calm.

6.2.2 Lucy learns to enjoy being handled by unfamiliar people too.

Fig. 6.2.2A

Fig. 6.2.2B

Fig. 6.2.2C

It's important for her to learn to enjoy letting others handler her too. When she goes to the veterinary hospital unfamiliar technicians and doctors may be treating her.

6.3 Giving Your Puppy Positive Experiences With Well-Behaved Dogs.

Giving your puppy positive experiences with many different dogs is an important part of socialization. But it's important that she interact only with appropriately behaved pets. For instance, interacting with a larger dog who just keeps pouncing on your puppy even though she screams can train her to be afraid of other dogs. In fact, when he was a puppy, my dad's last Cattle Dog was pounced on at the dog park on several occasions by a boisterous German Shepherd puppy. The Shepherd's owner shouted, "He's only playing." But my dad's Cattle Dog, who was screaming, was still terrified. After that, he was defensively aggressive to other dogs, especially German Shepherds.

Fig. 6.3A

Lucy's already met and played with seven new dogs in her first week with me. It's a good idea to set up play dates with vaccinated, well-behaved dogs. Lucy has been immediately comfortable with all of her dog visitors and solicited play with all of them without being too rough. Avoid letting your puppy play with dogs who are too rough, or she could learn to play in an overly aggressive manner. Also protect her from dogs who pounce on and scare her, or pester her when she tries to get away.

6.3.1 It's important to know when other dogs need a rest.

Not all dogs like to play, and while many like to play with their friends and other adult dogs, they may dislike pesky puppies. Or maybe they like playing a little, but not as much or as often as a pup.

Fig. 6.3.1A   Fig. 6.3.1B

Make sure the other dog wants to play. Here's Lucy and my dog, Jonesy. Both are off leash and Jonesy's clearly trying to avoid Lucy (Figure 6.3.1A). Then when she sticks her face in his mouth while he's complaining, that really sets him off (Figure 6.3.1B). He roars and bares his teeth and she ends up backing off (not shown here).

If she continues to bother him in spite of his warnings, I will distract her and reward her for more appropriate behavior, such as coming when called, and sitting and paying attention to me and then playing with a toy. If I continue to let her harass him and he always has to defend himself, I will be failing Jonesy by not intervening.

It's helpful to let well-behaved, experienced dogs teach puppies that a raised lip means to back off and the next step is a roar and a snap. But sometimes the older dog is not big enough or strong enough to make this message clear. Or the older dog may be intolerant and over-react. In either case, it's up to us to teach the puppy that when the other dog makes these signals, the pup should leave him alone and come to us because we call her.

Set the situation up so other pets can get away from the puppy

Fig. 6.3.1C

Fig. 6.3.1D

Fig. 6.3.1E

Here's a better play set-up. Now Lucy is on leash and tethered to a piece of furniture. She can still play, but Jonesy can play on his terms. When he wants to play, he comes over to her. Set the situation up so other pets can get away from the puppy.

Fig. 6.3.1F

When he wants a break, he can just walk away out of her reach.

Fig. 6.3.1G

Fig. 6.3.1H

Now they play in short bouts (Figures 6.2.1G) and then rest for a few seconds so they can both calm down (Figure 6.2.1H) and then start playing again. The play is always calm and relaxed. If the puppy yelps, play stops. If Jonesy needs a break, he stops or walks away.

6.4 Socializing the Puppy to Other Animals.

Lucy was already socialized to a cat in her first home.

Fig. 6.4A

Here I let her socialize with dog-friendly cats. If the she's too pushy, work on come when called. Remember, she should be on leash unless you're 100% sure she'll come when called. You can also give her treats for focusing on you or playing games with you near the cat, so she's not overly focused on the cat.

Fig. 6.4B

Fig. 6.4C

Later, I'll introduce her to livestock and get her to focus on me around animals in nature. The goal is that she can focus on me with all distractions and that she can be in close contact with other animals.

6.5 Making Your Puppy Comfortable in Many Different Environments.

Until your puppy is fully vaccinated, avoid parks and other locations where there might be unvaccinated dogs. Instead, walk on sidewalks and visit places where you know there will be no unvaccinated dogs.

Lucy's initially afraid of cars and tries to run the other way. We started in quiet areas and worked on repeated sit exercises and other games, as well as just letting her sit and watch the cars while giving her treats. By her third day, she's comfortable enough to watch them and eat treats—and to even ignore the car and pay attention only to the treats.

Fig. 6.5A

Fig. 6.5B

Fig. 6.5C

Here Lucy visits a car repair garage and hangs out in the waiting room, where she gets to play with the mechanics. It's important to socialize her to both men and women, and people of different ethnicities, energy levels and sizes.

6.6 Recognizing Fear and Anxiety in Dogs.
Modified from chapter 1 of *Low Stress Handling, Restraint and Behavior Modification of Dogs & Cats* (book and DVD)
www.lowstresshandling.com

People frequently socialize their puppy incorrectly by taking her out but not recognizing that the pup is not having a positive experience. It's important to be able to read your pup's emotional state, so you'll know if she's fearful or anxious. What follows is a kind of canine body language dictionary. You can download this handout/poster for free at www.drsophiayin.com.

Body Language of Fear in Dogs

Slight Cowering   **Major Cowering**

More Subtle Signs of Fear & Anxiety

Licking Lips
when no food nearby

Panting
when not hot or thirsty

Brow Furrowed, Ears to Side

Moving in Slow Motion
walking slow on floor

Acting Sleepy or Yawning
when they shouldn't be tired

Hypervigilant
looking in many directions

Suddenly Won't Eat
but was hungry earlier

Moving Away

Pacing

6.6.1 Brows and ears.

Fig. 6.6.1A
When scared, dogs hold their ears out to the side or back. They can also hold their ears in these positions for other reasons, so do not rely on ears alone to determine the dog's state of mind. When they are fearful, their brows show varying degrees of furrowing. In this picture, Jonesy, my Jack Russell Terrier, is fearful because he's afraid of riding in cars.

Fig. 6.6.1B
When holding a ball in front of this dog, his ears perk forward.

Fig. 6.6.1C
When he's being petted and enjoys it (which I know because he's rubbing against me), his ears go out and back slightly. Note that his brow is not furrowed. He's not fearful.

Fig. 6.6.1D
Here is his ear position when he's waiting for a treat. His ears are perked forward.

Fig. 6.6.1E
When he gets the treat and it's in his mouth or right in front of his nose, his ears go out slightly and back as his eyes try to focus on the tidbit near his nose. Note that his brow is not furrowed.

6.6.2 Licking lips.

Fig. 6.6.2A

Dogs lick their lips when they're nervous, or even excited. When it's nervousness, the licking is accompanied by other signs of fear as well.

6.6.3 He may stop eating.

Fig. 6.6.3A

A dog may stop eating, even treats, when he is nervous. Or he may grab the food more aggressively.

Fig. 6.6.3B

Now, several seconds later, he takes the treat that he refused earlier because he's a little less nervous. But he may go in and out of various states of fear.

6.6.4 Yawning and panting.

Fig. 6.6.4A
Anxious dogs may yawn when they are not tired.

Fig. 6.6.4B
And they may pant when they are not hot or thirsty.

6.6.5 She may act sleepy.

Fig. 6.6.5A

Fig. 6.6.5B

One of the most important early signs of fear is that the dog acts sleepy or lethargic (Figure 6.6.5A). Both of these dogs have their eyes partially closed and are moving slowly. This tired appearance (Figure 6.6.5B) can change from situation to situation or within seconds. When they are hypervigilant and moving in this sleepy way, they appear to be looking around in slow motion.

6.6.6 Cowering.

Fig. 6.6.6A

This dog is ducking to avoid being touched by an unfamiliar person. Overall, this dog leans away with his head and body lowered and his muscles tense. The dog's gaze is often averted, as if avoiding your eyes will keep you from seeing him, since a direct stare can be seen as a threat. If the dog's head is pointed away from you and he's still trying to look at you, you'll see the whites of his eyes (called whale eye). Also, his ears are often flat against his head and his tail is tucked beneath him. Cowering or running away are the most blatant signs of fear. Hopefully in most instances you recognize the more subtle signs first.

Dogs can show a cowering posture to different degrees.

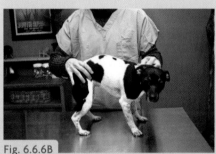

Fig. 6.6.6B

This dog is only cowering a little while standing. She is very tense though, which indicates that she is very nervous.

Fig. 6.6.4C

This dog is sitting, but she lowers her head as an unfamiliar person approaches because she's afraid of unfamiliar people. If the person fails to notice this slight cowering and continues walking forward, the dog will either cower more, or lunge, bark, and possibly bite in order to protect herself.

6.6.7 Cowering vs. submissive vs. affiliative gestures: an updated view of historically confusing terminology.

For many decades dog enthusiasts have been throwing the terminology describing body language and social behavior around carelessly—not out of maliciousness or laziness, but because this is how the terms were first used by scientists. Now, decades later, wolf biologists, comparative psychologists, and researchers studying canine social behavior have come to a clearer understanding of dogs and have, in turn revised some of the terminology that describes them. As with science in general, it often takes 10 or more years for the new information to trickle down to the general public. Here is the most updated information to date.

Cowering vs. Submissive Posture vs. Affiliative Gestures

Cowering: People sometimes equate cowering with submissive behavior and assume this behavior is good—that it means the dog is telling them he is willing to be subordinate to them. This interpretation is not quite correct. Dogs cower when they are afraid. It could be due to fear of punishment, a loud noise, or an unfamiliar, person, object, or dog that they perceive as scary.

Submissive or de-escalating postures: The actual definition of a submissive posture is one that it intended to turn off aggression and signal that the dog offering the signals will not fight—at least if the other dog (or person) reacts appropriately by stopping his assault. Hence submissive postures are now referred to by some scientists as de-escalating postures. These postures may or may not be driven by fear. For instance when playing with a friend, if one dog gets too rough and the other indicates it's irritation by growling, the instigator may get down low but most likely in a relaxed manner. This posture signals clearly that he is backing off. If the instigator lowers her body to the ground and is tense, trembling or suddenly moves in slow motion, this indicates fear. In both cases the appropriate response from the growling dog is to stop the threat too.

Affiliative gestures: Sometimes similar low body postures are exhibited in the absence of a threat. For instance, some dogs naturally greet other dogs and people by approaching with a low posture or even by lying down. Their body is relaxed though, their ears slightly back, and their tail or even their entire rear end is wagging. They often lick the other dog, especially on the side of the mouth the way a puppy might in order to solicit food. This is an affiliative gesture—one that promotes bonding. These postures are also called appeasement gestures; however the term "appeasement" can be confusing since some dictionary definitions for appeasement can overlap with the definition for submissive. I prefer referring to the postures in this type of context as affiliative.

Some dogs are more likely to exhibit affiliative postures than others. A highly gregarious dog may perform these gestures regularly when he greets new dogs or he may perform them primarily with dogs he's well-bonded with. Dogs may also direct affiliative behavior towards people if they are highly attracted to people.

Affiliative Gestures

Fig. 6.6.7A

This dog Niko loves playing with other dogs. At the dog park he goes up to dogs and greets in this manner. It generally results fairly quickly in mutual play. Dogs that run up to Niko quickly cause him to roll on his back. After they have sniffed him he gets up and runs away with his tail tucked between his legs. This belly-up display is a submissive behavior, one offered by the dog in order to turn off potential aggression. As a result, it would be appropriate to call it a submissive roll.

Fig. 6.6.7B

Niko also loves socializing with people and greets them with the same affiliative posture.

Fig. 6.6.7C

Here's Lucy as a grown-up. Lucy loves my dog, Jonesy, whom she probably considers her older brother. Whenever she is reunited with him, she gets to his level and licks his face, but she also sometimes jumps on him in play. Jonesy does not particularly love Lucy to the extent that she loves him, but he generally puts up with her affiliative behavior. Lucy loves humans, including unfamiliar people. She greets humans with this affiliative display too.

Although the low body posture and licking are affiliative gestures in the contexts and cases described above, dogs who are uncomfortable meeting new dogs or those who do not already have a relationship with the friendly individual may dislike being approached in this exuberant manner because it invades their personal space. It's similar to having a stranger or casual acquaintance approach too closely and then hover around

6.6.8 Hypervigilance.

Fearful dogs may frequently glance in different directions and for short time periods, the same way you might keep looking around for danger if you were walking alone in a bad neighborhood late at night and thought someone might be following you. Owners frequently think their fearful dog is just watching the scenery, when actually he is scanning for danger.

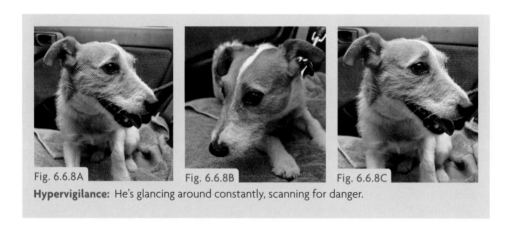

Fig. 6.6.8A   Fig. 6.6.8B   Fig. 6.6.8C

Hypervigilance: He's glancing around constantly, scanning for danger.

How Does Fear Become Aggression?

Fearful dogs can easily learn that offense is the best defense. Rather than fleeing or freezing when they are fearful, they believe they should attack—sometimes even before the object or person or dog has a chance to get close. These dogs still show signs of anxiety and fear, such as averting their gaze, hiding and backing up. But these signs of anxiety may be fleeting as they put up a strong front. They are likely to show anxious signs in other circumstances though.

This dog adopts a highly aroused posture when he sees objects such as brooms that startle him and scare him. He's tense, leaning forward, tail and head held high and ears forward initially, when the object is far enough away. As the object comes closer, he will show fear postures and back away.

Fig. 6.6.7D

6.7 What to Do If You Notice Signs of Fear and Anxiety in Your Puppy.

If you notice signs of fear or anxiety in your puppy, the goal is to change her emotional state to happy. You can do so by doing things that make her happy, such as feeding a steady stream of treats so she doesn't have a chance to think about how scared she is. Or you can have her perform behaviors that are fun. You have a bunch you've worked on already—repeat sits, come when called. You must do them in rapid succession to prevent her from thinking about the scary thing.

6.7.1 Why to avoid forcing your puppy to face her fears.

Some people may think that if your dog is fearful you should just place her in the fear-inducing situation so she gets used to it. This can work in cases where the puppy's fear is not intense and even in some cases where it is. But it can also be associated with some major side effects.

Avoid trying to handle the scary situation by just holding her down as the "danger" approaches. This might work if the fear is minor. But it can also backfire and make the fear much worse. Why?

Fig. 6.7.1A
Imagine you were afraid of spiders and someone put this close to you.

Fig. 6.7.1B
Now imagine they held you down while holding the spider close to you.

A better approach is to work at a distance where you can keep the puppy in a happy emotional state and focused on you. Then, systematically work your way closer to the scary object. When you are confident about staying at the level where she's happy and focused you can improve quickly. Not that the better your technique at the various exercises, the faster your puppy will improve. Then, systematically work your way closer to the scary object.

6.7.2 When to get help.

Because fears can progress to aggression, if your puppy shows fears that don't immediately improve when you try these techniques, you should seek professional help. (Look for a qualified behaviorist at www.AVSABonline.org, www.dacvb.org, or www. animalbehaviorsociety.org) For more information on behavior modification of fearful pets refer to *Low Stress Handling, Restraint and Behavior Modification of Dog & Cats* (book and DVD) at www.lowstresshandling.com.

6.8 Checklist for Socialization.

The goals of socialization are that the puppy has positive experiences, not neutral or bad ones. It's important to watch the puppy's response and note what it is and to also give treats to help ensure the exposure is a success. Here's a checklist that can help you. Download a copy of this puppy socialization checklist at www.drsophiayin.com.

You can grade the response if you want or just check off each exposure.

PROGRESS	SCORE	RESPONSE TO THE PERSON, OBJECT, ENVIRONMENT OR HANDLING
Needs Work	1	**Overarousal or try to get at:** Growl, nip, bark, struggle (for handling), or lunge
	2	**Avoid:** Struggle, hide, try to get away, won't approach, or hesitant to approach
	3	**Freeze:** Holds still (but not eating), non-exploratory, moving slowly or acting sleepy when they shouldn't be tired
Going well	4	**Calm, relaxed,** explores the object or environment, playful, **focused on the food**
	5	Calm, relaxed, explores the object or environment, playful, **even without food**

Additionally a + can be used to denote better progress and a – denotes not as well (e.g. 2+, 2, 2-) such that each score can include three levels of response.

Week Start Date _____

CLASS OF SOCIALIZATION	SPECIFIC SOCIALIZATION	DAY & SCORE (or check mark)						
		M	T	W	Th	F	S	Sun
Handling 	Checking the ears							
	Examining mouth and gums							
	Opening the eyelids							
	Squeezing the feet							
	Handling and trimming the toenails							
	Pinching skin							
	Poking the skin with a capped pen							
	Touching and squeezing the nose							
	Poking the nose with a capped pen							
	Cradling puppy in your arms on its back							
	Holding him in your lap							
	Holding puppy upside down							
	Holding puppy on its back while giving a belly rub							
	Hugging your puppy							
	Pulling the collar (gotcha)							
	Grabbing puppy by other part of body							
	Wiping body with a towel							
	Putting on a head halter							
	Putting on a harness							

Week Start Date _____

CLASS OF SOCIALIZATION	SPECIFIC SOCIALIZATION	M	T	W	Th	F	S	Sun
Unfamiliar People	Women							
	People of many ethnicities							
	Tall men							
	Men with deep voices							
	Men with beards							
	Elderly							
	People wearing hats, helmets							
	People wearing Ugg® boots							
	People wearing hoodies							
	People wearing backpacks							
	People wearing sunglasses							
	People with canes, walking sticks or walkers							
	Teenagers							
	Children standing as well as playing							
	Toddlers (walking and squealing)							
	Infants (crawling)							
	People running by							
	Indigent or homeless people							
Unfamiliar Dogs	Dogs who play well							
	A dog who will reprimand puppies with appropriate force and restraint for getting into his personal space							
	With puppies who play well and do not get overly aroused							

DAY & SCORE (or check mark)

157

Week Start Date _____

CLASS OF SOCIALIZATION	SPECIFIC SOCIALIZATION	DAY & SCORE (or check mark)						
		M	T	W	Th	F	S	Sun
Other animal species	Cats							
	Horses and livestock							
	Any types of pets you may have							
New surfaces	Concrete							
	Slippery floors such as hardwood, linoleum or marble							
	Metal surfaces-such as manhole covers, vet hospital scales							
	Wobbly surfaces such as BOSU® ball, a board on top of a book or unbalanced thick tree branch, a wobble board							
	Stairs							
	Wet grass							
	Mud							
	Ice, frost, or snow if you will live in such areas							
Scary sounds If you do not have the ability to expose the puppy to these sounds frequently enough or at a level where she can have a positive experience, use sound CDs. Some sounds may be more realistic when surround sound is used.	Thunder							
	Fireworks							
	Babies and kids							
	Alarms							
	Dogs barking							
	Doorbell wringing							
	Traffic (like downtown in a city)							
	Jack hammers							
	Vacuum cleaner							
	Sirens							

Week Start Date _____

CLASS OF SOCIALIZATION	SPECIFIC SOCIALIZATION	DAY & SCORE (or check mark)						
		M	T	W	Th	F	S	Sun
Objects with wheels	Skateboards							
	Rollerblades							
	Garbage cans outside							
	Shopping carts							
	Baby strollers							
	Wheel chairs							
	Bikes							
	Cars							
	Buses							
	Motorcycles							
Man-made objects	Pots and pans							
	Blankets or rugs being shaken							
	Brooms							
	Balloons							
	Umbrellas							
	Bags blowing in the wind							
	Sidewalk signs							
	Garbage cans in the house							
	Garbage cans outside							
	Plastic bags blowing the wind							
	Large plastic garbage bags							
	Metal pans or other metal surfaces							
	Metal-pens							

Week Start Date —————————————————————

CLASS OF SOCIALIZATION	SPECIFIC SOCIALIZATION	DAY & SCORE (or check mark)						
		M	T	W	Th	F	S	Sun
New environments	Suburban neighborhood							
	Residential city streets							
	High traffic city street (such as downtown)							
	Shopping mall parking lot							
	Inside buildings							
	Dog-friendly event such as an agility or obedience trial							
	Location of several different dog training classes							

Chapter 7

A Head Start on All the Rest

Well, that's pretty much all you need to know to get your puppy off to a perfect start. Since Lucy learned so quickly, she learned a few more things, too. Here are a few more exercises. »

7.1 Learning to Lie Down.

We'll start this by using a piece of food to lure Lucy into the down position. Then I'll show you how to add a verbal cue and a hand signal.

7.1.1 Using a food lure.

Fig. 7.1.1A   Fig. 7.1.1B

STEP 1 | **Using a food lure:** Start with a food lure in your right hand. Hold the lure up to the puppy's nose.

Fig. 7.1.1C

STEP 2 | **Then move the treat towards the ground.** Move slowly enough so that the puppy keeps her nose on your hand as you lower it.

Fig. 7.1.1D

STEP 3 | **Lower the treat to the ground.** Her nose should still be in contact with the treat.

NOTE: At first, many puppies need to receive the treat lure as a reward when they're just halfway bent to the ground or they'll get up.

Fig. 7.1.1E

STEP 4 | **Slide the treat out:** Once the treat is on the ground slide it away from the puppy slightly so that her nose moves forward a little and she has room to lie down. Once she's lying down give her the treat and a few additional ones for remaining down.

7.1.2 Graduate to a hand signal and later a verbal cue.

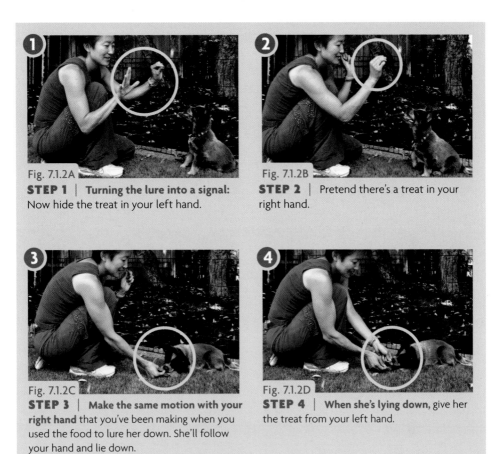

Fig. 7.1.2A
STEP 1 | **Turning the lure into a signal:** Now hide the treat in your left hand.

Fig. 7.1.2B
STEP 2 | Pretend there's a treat in your right hand.

Fig. 7.1.2C
STEP 3 | **Make the same motion with your right hand** that you've been making when you used the food to lure her down. She'll follow your hand and lie down.

Fig. 7.1.2D
STEP 4 | **When she's lying down,** give her the treat from your left hand.

To add the verbal cue, say "down" just before you give her the hand signal to lie down. Remember that the word must come before the hand signal or she won't pay attention to the word. Also be sure that you don't add the verbal cue until she consistently lies down with the hand signal within one second, using the hand signal alone. Otherwise she'll learn that the verbal cue means nothing.

7.2 Learning to Go From a Down to a Sit.

I added this exercise because for some reason my dad felt it was very important. He specifically asked me to train a sit from the down position.

7.2.1 First with a food lure.

Fig. 7.2.1A   Fig. 7.2.1B

From down to sit: Hold the treat in your left hand while the puppy is lying down. Put the treat in front of the pup's nose (Figure 7.2.1A). Then lift your hand up so that she jumps up into a sit to get it (Figure 7.2.1B). When she immediately goes into a sit consistently when you do this, you're ready to switch to using the left hand as a signal instead of a lure.

7.2.2 Graduate to a hand signal and later a verbal cue.

Fig. 7.2.2A

STEP 1 | **Hold your left palm out** and hide the treat in your right hand so it doesn't distract the puppy. Start with your left hand by your side.

Fig. 7.2.2B

STEP 2 | **Then raise your left hand** the way you raised it when you were holding the treat.

Fig. 7.2.2C

STEP 3 | **Reward her once she sits.** Because the puppy has moved into a sit so many times to get a treat from your left hand, she should sit up with just the hand signal. Quickly reward her with a treat from your right hand so she remains sitting.

Fig. 7.2.2D

NOTE: Most people don't give such a prominent sit cue. The reason we are using this cue where you raise your arm so it's 90° like a right turn signal is that your dog will be able to see this cue clearly even when

If you want to teach the verbal cue "sit," just say "sit" right before you give the hand signal so that it will predict the hand signal. If you give them simultaneously, it will take longer for her to learn the verbal cue because it will not predict anything for her.

7.3 Training the Down-stay Using the MannersMinder® (a.k.a. Treat&Train).

The only major behavior that most people will want to train but that we have not worked on much yet is the down-stay—although you have started it during some of the other exercises by rewarding the puppy several times in a row for remaining lying down. The quick way to teach a down-stay and to reward dogs while they are calmly lying down is with the MannersMinder® (a.k.a. Treat&Train®). Because the rewards are activated by remote control you can reward the dog when he is lying down away from you such as on the other side of the room.

The MannersMinder® comes with a timer function that tells you when to dole out treats. At first you reward frequently—every several seconds as long as the dog remains lying down. Then you systematically and rapidly increase the interval between treats so that the dog is waiting in a down-stay longer and longer for each treat. Because of the systematic nature of the training protocol and the precise timing that occurs when treats are dispensed remotely, the down-stay can easily be trained within a few days to a few weeks depending on the amount of the dog's meal you will use and the type of distractions you're working with. Best of all you can do the training while you're watching T.V. or working on other tasks.

Fig. 7.3A   Fig. 7.3B

Training a down-stay with the MannersMinder® a.k.a. Treat & Train (Premier Pet Products®; www.MannersMinder.net). Jonesy demonstrates a down-stay using the MannersMinder®, an automatic treat dispenser that you can control remotely. This product comes with a DVD with step-by-step instruction for training dogs to lie down and remain calm in situations where they might otherwise bark, jump, whine or be anxious or unruly. With this program we can teach a basic down-stay in as little as a couple of days. With Lucy I'll use it to train her to lie down on a rug and wait patiently with distractions such as when visitors come to the door. I'll also use it to train her to do a down-stay while I'm training Jonesy or to reward Jonesy for patiently lying down in one place while I train Lucy.

7.4 Improving Communication by Teaching a Marker Sound or Bridging Stimulus.

Sometimes when training dogs and other animals it can difficult to get the treat to the animal while or immediately after the animal performs the correct behavior. Because the timing of the reward is late, the animal doesn't understand which behavior earned the reward. To improve our ability to communicate the desired behavior to our puppy we can train a marker sound, otherwise known as a bridging stimulus. That is, we can pair food with a unique sound like the click from a toy clicker, or a word they rarely hear, such as "yes" spoken in a distinct, sharp tone. By producing the sound and immediately following with food repeatedly, the puppy will learn that the sound predicts that the food treat is coming. Once this association is established, the sound can be used to tell the puppy exactly when he is performing a correct behavior. The puppy knows that when he hears the sound, whatever he was doing at the time has earned him a reward. In other words, the sound comes to bridge the gap between the desired behavior and the food reinforcer.

Fig. 7.4A

Clickers are commonly used as markers or bridging stimuli because they have a distinct sound that stand out in the environment. By pairing the clicker with food you can teach the dog that the click sound predicts that they've done something correct and will get a reward. Sounds or words that are indistinct or that have been used frequently without immediate pairing with a high value reward make poor markers because dogs don't notice them or have already learned that these sounds predict nothing.

> *"A marker sound is a sound that has been paired with something the dog likes, such as food, enough times that the dog understands that when he hears the sound, it means a food reward is coming."*

7.4.1 Training the marker sound or bridging stimulus.

Fig. 7.4.1A   Fig. 7.4.1B

How to train the marker sound or bridging stimulus: The MannersMinder® (a.k.a. Treat & Train®) uses a tone as a marker or bridging stimulus. To train Lucy that this tone means a treat is coming, I first put food in the MannersMinder® bowl so she knows that food sometimes appears in the bowl. Once she has figured this out and readily eats the kibble I'm using as treats, I press the remote control so that a tone sounds and the MannersMinder® immediately dispenses a kibble into the bowl. I dispense treats repeatedly at varying intervals, sometimes a treat every couple of seconds and sometime treats spaced at longer intervals such as between 5-10 seconds as long as Lucy sticks close enough to the MannersMinder® to see that treats are being dispensed.

Within several minutes, even if she is looking away from the MannersMinder®, when Lucy hears the beep, she turns to the MannersMinder® to get her food reward (Figures 7.4.1A and B). You know that an animal understands the association if they are looking away from the MannersMinder® yet immediately orient to and approach the device when they hear the tone.

Practice Tips

- When training the sound-treat association, the interval at which you deliver both can be important. Dogs often learn the sound-treat association best when the sound and food are presented at irregular intervals. If the food comes frequently and at regular intervals, the tone is not important as a predictor for when the food will arrive.

7.4.2 Using the marker to train behaviors efficiently.

Fig. 7.4.2A   Fig. 7.4.2B

Mark and reward attention: Once dogs understand this tone-reward association, it is easy to switch to specifically teaching the dog that focusing on you earns rewards. I demonstrate this training with Jonesy. Just press the remote when he's quiet and looking at you. First reward him immediately when he looks at you. But when the dog is good at this, require that he look at you for slightly longer periods of attention before you reward him by pressing the remote. This is a good exercise for teaching dogs to remain calm and focused on you instead of pawing or barking at the MannersMinder®.

Fig. 7.4.2C   Fig. 7.4.2D

Shaping targeting behavior. Once I taught Lucy the tone-treat association, the next step was to teach her to touch a target with here nose. I trained this behavior through a process called shaping. That is, I started by rewarding a behavior I could get and then systematically rewarded behaviors closer and closer to my goal behavior. At first when I presented the target near her face I sounded the tone so she got a treat when she just looked at the target (a red foam ball on the end of a stick) and upon hearing the tone she would turn back to the MannersMinder® to get her treat.

Fig. 7.4.2E
Fig. 7.4.2F

Rewarding the goal behavior. Once Lucy was good at looking at the target, I'd only trigger the remote when she stretched her neck to touch the target. Once she was readily touching the target with her nose I started requiring she take a few steps to touch the target. Here she actually touches the target with her open mouth and then turns to get her food reward when she hears the beep. If I want her to touch with her nose and not her open mouth, I"ll have to reward only touches with her nose.

7.4.3 Markers and shaping come in handy for training complex behaviors.

Shaping and the use of a marker can come in handy for training many complex behaviors—especially those where the dog may be looking away from you, far away from you, or where it's otherwise difficult to get the reward to the animal exactly as he's performing the correct behavior.

Fig. 7.4.3A

Jonesy's karate kick was trained with a clicker as a marker. At first I just clicked and treated when he lifted the right hind leg a little. Then I sequentially click-treated higher leg raises and then high leg raises followed by a kick. Without a clicker this trick would have been much harder to train because it would have been hard to get the reward to him while his leg was still in the air rather than when it was back on the ground. As a result he would not have been able to figure out which behavior was supposed to earn rewards.

Fig. 7.4.3B

Jonesy also learned to play fetch using a clicker because he was not reliably interested in toys or balls. I started by clicking and treating when he looked at the tennis ball I was holding in my hand. When he could perform this behavior quickly about five to 10 times in a row, then I only click-treated when he touched the tennis ball with his nose. Then with the next sequence of steps I started holding the ball lower so that it was closer to the ground. Once he would reliable run and touch the ball on the ground, I started click-treating only when he put his mouth on the ball and then later when he grabbed the ball. And finally I started rewarding for picking it up and carrying it one step towards me, then, two, then three, then four steps, until he got to the point where he could deliver it all the way and drop it into my hand. While this seems like a lot of steps, by working in a systematic manner, Jonesy was able to learn to fetch in just a couple of days. That's partly because Jack Russell Terriers are so energetic that they can drill on the same behavior many times in a short period. The more repetitions they can get in a session (while they are still enjoying the training) the faster they can learn the behavior. That's why many Jack Russell Terriers can learn so many tricks so quickly compared to dogs that move more slowly or get tired sooner.

The possibilities for training are endless when a bridging stimulus and shaping are used.

Fig. 7.4.3C

Fig. 7.4.3D

Fig. 7.4.3E

Putting toys away. Here Jonesy demonstrates his ability to put his toys away, happily. Dogs who already know to pick up toys or to fetch can learn this behavior in just a few sessions.

Fig. 7.4.3F

Fig. 7.4.3G

Fig. 7.4.3H

Fig. 7.4.3I

Putting paper in the recycle bin. As a variation on the exercise shown earlier, dogs can easily be taught other useful behavior such as putting paper into the recycle bin.

7.4 Conclusion.

Well, that's it! The secret to having a perfect puppy in a week.

I started with an outgoing, playful puppy who loved to jump, nip, and could do so with boundless energy. After a week I had the same outgoing, playful puppy but she automatically sat politely for everything she wanted, walked nicely on leash, was comfortable with being handled for basic care, and directed her play towards appropriate toys and games such as fetch. Although she was still insecure in high traffic environments, she was comfortable around and enjoyed playing with many types of well-mannered canine and human visitors. With continued positive experiences she will continue to improve and with consistent training, her polite behaviors will become a permanent habit, even with my parents.

Realistically, Lucy was perfect so quickly because I already knew the techniques for training her and could ensure that all household members and visitors followed the rules. For you, it may take a little longer, because you're learning at the same time your dog is. Plus, it may take some effort to train all of the human family members too. Additionally, even with this book, you'll want to enroll your puppy in at least one series of puppy socialization classes where its easy to find the people, puppies, and environmental set-ups for socializing her. Nevertheless, with what you've learned here, you can train your puppy faster than you ever though possible.

Of course, the next question for Lucy is: Will my senior citizen parents be willing and able to follow the same training plan?

Stay tuned for the next book!

References

American Veterinary Society of Animal Behavior.2007. AVSAB Position Statement: The use of punishment for dealing with animal behavior problems. www.AVSABonline.org

American Veterinary Society of Animal Behavior.2008. AVSAB Position Statement On Puppy Socialization. The use of punishment for dealing with animal behavior problems. www.AVSABonline.org

Beaver, B. 2009. Canine Behavior of Sensory and Neural Origin. *Canine Behavior: Issues and Answers* St Louis: Saunders

Bradshaw, J.W.S. 2011. Dog Sense: How the New Science of Dog Behavior Can Make You a Better Friend to Your Pet. New York: Basic Books

Bradshaw J.W.S, C.E. Cooke, N. C. E. Robertson and W.J. Browne. *Competitive relationships among a colony of 1 castrated male domestic dogs.* Manuscript submitted for publication.

Jacobs, G.H. and J.F. Deegan II, M.A. Crognale, and J.A. Febnwick. 1993. Photopigments of dogs and foxes and their implications for canid vision. *Vis Neurosci* 10: 173-180.

Miklósi, Á. 2007. Dog Behaviour, Evolution and Cognition. Oxford, New York: Oxford University Press.

Miller, Paul E and Christopher J. Murphy. 1995. Vision in dogs. *Journal of the American Veterinary Medical Association,* 207:12, pp. 1623-1634.

Neitz, J., T. Geist, and G.H. Jacobs. 1989. Color vision in the dog. *Visual Neuroscience* 3: 119-125.

Neitz, J., E. Carroll, M. Neitz. 2001. Color vision: Almost reason enough for having eyes. *Optics and Photonic News.* 12: 26-33.

Packard, J.M.., 2003. Wolf Behavior: Reproductive, Social and Intelligent. 2003. In *Wolves Behavior, Ecology and Conservation,* ed, .D. Mech and L. Boitani, 51-52. Chicago: Chicago University Press.

Pelar, C., 2005. Living with Kids and Dogs... Without Losing Your Mind: A Parent's Guide to Controlling the Chaos. Woodbridge, VA: C & R Publishing, LLC

Scott, J.P. and J.L. Fuller. 1965.Genetics and the Social Behavior of the Dog. Chicago: University of Chicago Press.

Walker, D.B., J.C. Walker, P.J. Cavnar, J.L. Taylor, D.H. Pickel, S. B. Hall, and J.C. Suarez. 2006. Naturalistic quantification of canine olfactory sensitivity. *Applied Animal Behaviour Science –* 97:2, pp. 241-254.

Yin, S.Y. 2009. Low Stress Handling, Restraint, and Behavior Modification of Dogs & Cats. Davis: CattleDog Publishing.

About the Author

Dr. Sophia Yin is a veterinarian and applied animal behaviorist, with a passion for helping people understand animals and their behavior. Voted one of the *Bark Magazine's* 100 Best and Brightest, she has been producing cutting edge educational materials for over 20 years. She is the author of several books and textbooks, including *How to Behave So Your Dog Behaves, Low Stress Handling, Restraint and Behavior Modification of Dogs & Cats* (book and DVD), and *The Small Animal Veterinary Nerdbook®*, a best-selling textbook for veterinary students.

Dr. Yin graduated from the UC Davis School of Veterinary Medicine in 1993 and later earned her Master's in Animal Science in 2001 from UC Davis where she studied vocal communication in dogs and worked on behavior modification in horses, giraffes, ostriches, and chickens. During this time she was also the award-winning pet columnist for The San Francisco Chronicle. Upon receiving her degree focused on animal behavior, Dr. Yin served for five years as a guest lecturer in the UC Davis Animal Science Department. She taught three upper division undergraduate courses in domestic animal behavior and supervised students in various animal training and behavior research projects. She also developed the Manners Minder (a.k.a. Treat and Train) remote controlled, positive reinforcement dog training system (www. MannersMinder.net).

Dr. Yin currently owns and operates a house calls practice for pets with behavioral problems, works at San Francisco Veterinary Specialists (www.SFVS.net), runs a popular web site with free behavior information, (www.drsophiayin.com), has consulted for several zoos, lectures internationally on animal behavior, and has served as a behavior expert for shows such as Dogs 101 on Animal Planet. She is also on the executive board for the American Veterinary Society of Animal Behavior and was a member of the American Association of Feline Practitioners (AAFP) Handling Guidelines Committee. For more information on Dr. Yin and on animal behavior visit her site at www. drsophiayin.com.

Visit Dr. Yin's web site for access to **FREE** animal behavior information and downloads, drsophiayin.com.

Download free educational posters, handouts and e-newsletters:

View over 40 short videos and read hundreds of blog articles:

Check out her other behavior books and products:

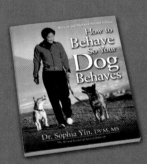 

Find information on your pet's behavioral issues on her Dog Behavior and Training Issues Page **drsophiayin.com/resources**

Great Tools That Help Develop Great Dogs